HEY LONG ISLAND...

Do U Remember?

Stacy Mandel Kaplan   **Kimberly Towers**

Scott J. Mandel   **Jordan Kaplan**

MacIntyre Purcell Publishing Inc.
Lunenburg, Nova Scotia

MacIntyre Purcell Publishing Inc.
194 Hospital Rd.
Lunenburg, Nova Scotia
B0J 2C0
(902) 640-3350

www.macintyrepurcell.com
info@macintyrepurcell.com

Printed and bound in Canada by Friesens

Cover design: Gwen North
Book design: Gwen North

Front cover: Montauk Point Lighthouse, photo by Kathleen Balsamo.
Back cover: Long Beach Boardwalk, photo courtesy of Long Beach Historical and Preservation Society; New York Islanders Parade, photo courtesy of Carol Silva; Nunley's Carousel, photo by Denise Rafkind.

ISBN: 978-1-77276-169-6

Library and Archives Canada Cataloguing in Publication
Title: Hey Long Island... : do u remember? / Stacy Mandel Kaplan, Kimberly Towers, Scott J. Mandel, Jordan Kaplan.
Names: Mandel Kaplan, Stacy, author. | Towers, Kimberly, author. | Mandel, Scott J., author. | Kaplan, Jordan (Jordan Ira), author.
Identifiers: Canadiana 20220140790 | ISBN 9781772761696 (hardcover)
Subjects: LCSH: Long Island (N.Y.)—History. | LCSH: Long Island (N.Y.)—History—Pictorial works. | LCSH: Long Island (N.Y.)—History—Anecdotes.
Classification: LCC F127.L8 M36 2022 | DDC 974.7/21—dc23

ABOUT LONG ISLAND

Geography

Long Island is located in the southeast part of the state of New York. It spans 0.35 miles east of Manhattan Island at New York Harbor and extends eastward over 100 miles into the Atlantic Ocean. Its land area is 1,401 square miles.

From the west, Long Island is separated from the island of Manhattan and the Bronx by the East River. At its northern borders, it is separated from Westchester County and the state of Connecticut by the Long Island Sound, and northeast from Rhode Island by the Block Island Sound. To the southwest, it is separated from Staten Island and the state of New Jersey by Upper New York Bay, the Narrows, and Lower New York Bay. To the south and to the east is the Atlantic Ocean.

"Long Island" generally refers to the main island and its surrounding outer barrier islands. These include Fire, Plum, Robins, Gardiners, Fishers, Long Beach Barrier, Jones Beach, Great Gull, Little Gull, and Shelter Islands.

Long Island is the 11th-largest island in the United States, the 149th-largest island in the world and is larger than the smallest U.S. state, Rhode Island. Long Island is the most populous island in any U.S. state or territory.

Counties

Long Island consists of four counties. Nassau County shares the western third of the island with the boroughs of Queens County and Kings County (Brooklyn). The eastern two-thirds of the island make up Suffolk County.

The "Nassau-Suffolk" definition of Long Island does not have any legal existence, but it is recognized as a "region" by the state of New York. People in the New York metropolitan area colloquially use the term Long Island (or the Island) to refer exclusively to Nassau and Suffolk counties, and conversely, refer to "the City" as Manhattan.

Island Status

In 1985, the U.S. Supreme Court in *United States v. Maine*, (also known as the Rhode Island and New York Boundary Case), held that Long Island was an extension of the mainland, not an island. The case involved a dispute as to which entity, the states or the federal government, controlled the Long Island and Block Island Sounds or inland bays. The states sought to gain control to regulate shipping and commerce. The Court ruled in favor of the states, and it was determined that the East River, which separates Long Island from the mainland, was too shallow for safe ship passage until humans widened it. Therefore, Long Island could not be considered a natural island. The Court also found that Long Island and the adjacent shore shared a common geological history. However, the United States Board on Geographic Names still considers Long Island an island, because it is surrounded by water.

LONG ISLAND THROUGH THE YEARS

Photo by Kathleen Balsamo.

19,000 BC: Long Island is formed by a glacier
Long Island, as part of the Outer Lands region, is formed largely of two spines of glacial moraine, with a large, sandy outwash plain beyond. These moraines consist of gravel and loose rock left behind during the two most recent pulses of Wisconsin glaciation during the ice ages some 21,000 years ago.

Before 1640: The original 13 Native American Tribes lived on Long Island "Paumanok"
The Canarsee, Rockaway, Merrick, Marsapeague, Secatogue, and Unkechaug lived on the South Shore. The Matinecock, Nesaquake, Setalcott, and Corchaug lived on the North Shore. On the east end of the Island were the Shinnecock, Manhasset, and the Montauks. Paumanok is a Native American name for Long Island meaning "The Island that Pays Tribute."

October 21, 1640: Long Island's first town
There is controversy about the earliest town on Long Island. The very first European settlements on Long Island were by settlers from England and from its colonies in present-day New England. Lion Gardiner settled nearby Gardiners Island. The first settlement on Long Island itself was on October 21, 1640, when Southold was established by the Rev. John Youngs and settlers from New Haven, Connecticut. Peter Hallock is considered the first New World settler on Long Island as he was granted the honor to step ashore first. However, Southampton claims the Halsey House was settled even earlier and that it is indeed the earliest town.

1658: Deep Hollow Ranch, the oldest cattle ranch in the United States, is founded
The oldest cattle ranch in the United States and self-proclaimed birthplace of the American cowboy is in Montauk County Park.

1683: The establishment of the NY Counties of Kings, Suffolk, and Queens
...but it is not what you think. When first established, Queens County included western Long Island, as well as the present-day towns of Hempstead and Oyster Bay.

November 5, 1796: The Montauk Point Lighthouse is completed
The Montauk Point Lighthouse is the oldest lighthouse in New York State.

May 31, 1819: Walt Whitman is born
Best known for his beloved poetry collection *Leaves of Grass*, Whitman was born in West Hills.

1826: Fire Island Lighthouse is completed
Fire Island hosts the tallest lighthouse on Long Island.

April 24, 1834: The Long Island Rail Road (LIRR)
Chartered on April 24, 1834, and operating continuously ever since, it is the oldest railroad in the United States that still operates under its original charter and name.

January 1, 1898: Queens County becomes part of New York City
All the western towns in Queens County officially became part of New York City.

January 1, 1899: Nassau County established
The County of Nassau was established, separate from and east of the counties of New York City.

1902 – 1908: Sagamore Hill, Oyster Bay
This 23-room, Victorian-styled home was President Theodore Roosevelt's "Summer White House." It exists today as a museum and a park.

1914: Long Beach Boardwalk is built
With the ocean on one side and the bay on the other, Long Beach developed as a seaside community. A 2.25-mile-long oceanfront boardwalk was built in 1914 with the help of circus elephants to haul and lay timbers.

April 10, 1925: F. Scott Fitzgerald's first publication of *The Great Gatsby*
The Gold Coast of Long Island plays its own role in this historical novel. Gatsby's fictional bayside villages of West Egg and East Egg represent the real-life communities of Great Neck (West Egg) and Port Washington (East Egg).

May 20, 1927: Charles Lindbergh's solo flight from Roosevelt Field
Charles Lindbergh lifted off from Roosevelt Field in his *Spirit of Saint Louis* for a historic solo flight to Europe. This was the event that helped establish Long Island as an early center of aviation during the 20th century.

July 28, 1929: Jacqueline Kennedy Onassis is born
Former First Lady, Jacqueline Kennedy Onassis, was born in Southampton.

December 6, 1929: Grumman Corporation started in Baldwin
Grumman was one of the most important builders of military aircraft in the 20th century, and it all began in a small garage in Baldwin.

1931: The Big Duck
The Big Duck off Route 24 in Flanders was originally built by a duck farmer named Martin Maurer as a place to sell his duck eggs.

1937: Grumman moves to Bethpage
Unlike many companies after the Great Depression, Grumman increased its factory size and workforce, and would become one of the major employers on Long Island.

1938: Valley Stream Teachers Federal Credit Union is founded
Valley Stream Teachers Federal Credit Union was founded in 1938 to serve teachers in the area of Valley Stream. In 1981, it became Nassau Educators Federal Credit Union (NEFCU) and on September 23, 2019, it re-branded as Jovia Financial Credit Union.

1940: Nunley's opens in Baldwin
Nunley's carousel and amusement park was located in Baldwin from 1940 to 1995.

October 1, 1947: Levittown, the first modern American suburb
Known as the nation's first planned community, Levittown was built for returning World War II veterans. Suburbia was transformed by mass-produced homes that emphasized conformity and uniformity.

Photo courtesy of Michael White.

Photo by Kevin Mazur.

Photo by Bill Barash.

1962: Adventureland opens in Farmingdale
To satisfy a growing appetite for family entertainment, Long Island's full-scale amusement park opened with a variety of rides and attractions, including roller coasters, games, and a ferris wheel.

April 21, 1964 – October 21, 1965: World's Fair at Flushing Meadows–Corona Park in Queens
Opened in 1964 for two six-month seasons, the World's Fair was the largest ever held in the United States.

1965: Grandma pizza invented at Umberto's, New Hyde Park
A delicious tradition began when a third type of pizza was invented. It is neither thin and round, nor thick and square. Grandma pizza is a thin rectangular pizza slice, topped with cheese and tomato sauce, reminiscent of that made by grandmothers at home without a pizza oven.

March 26, 1968: Rev. Dr. Martin Luther King, Jr. visits
Rev. Dr. Martin Luther King, Jr. came to Long Island and spoke in Long Beach and Rockville Centre. He delivered speeches about his vision for the Civil Rights Movement and the Poor People's Campaign.

1969 – 1999: Oak Beach Inn (OBI), Jones Beach Island
This converted inn became a popular Long Island nightspot, serving up cocktails and political controversy.

May 9, 1949: William Martin Joel is born
Songwriter, singer, and musician Billy Joel is known for the Long Island themes that run throughout his iconic lyrics. Shortly after he was born, the family moved to a section of America's famous "first suburb," in the Levittown/Hicksville area of Long Island.

1950s: The Miracle Mile originates
The Miracle Mile is a prominent shopping district in Manhasset on the North Shore of Long Island. It consists of the area along Northern Boulevard between Community Drive to the west, and Port Washington Boulevard and Searingtown Road to the east.

June 26, 1952: Jones Beach Theater opens
Northwell Health at Jones Beach Theater (commonly known as the Jones Beach Theater) is an outdoor amphitheatre at Jones Beach State Park in Wantagh.

October 18, 1958: Invention of the first video game
The Brookhaven National Laboratory in Upton, Long Island, is the birthplace of the first video game. Invented by physicist William Higinbotham in 1958, the game was called *Tennis for Two*.

June 4, 1959: Nathan's Roadside Restaurant opens in Oceanside
Nathan Handwerker, founder of the famous Nathan's hot dog stand in Coney Island, Brooklyn, expanded his business to Oceanside, establishing a center of family dining and entertainment for decades to follow.

1970: Long Island Game Farm opens in Manorville
Long Island's animal wildlife park and children's zoo opened at the Novak Family home.

1972: Snapple is founded in Valley Stream
"Made from the Best Stuff on Earth." Originally known as Unadulterated Food Products, the beverage company was created to supply fruit juices to health food stores. "Snapple," a portmanteau derived from the words "snappy" and "apple," became the new name for the enterprise. Snapple is well-known for printing interesting facts on the inside of its bottle caps.

1972: Long Island Iced Tea is created
Robert "Rosebud" Butt worked at the Oak Beach Inn (OBI) when he allegedly invented Long Island Iced Tea. Butt claimed he created the recipe as an entry in a contest to invent a new mixed drink with triple sec.

February 11, 1972: Nassau Veterans Memorial Coliseum opens
The Nassau Coliseum opened as the home of both the Nets and the Islanders. The $32-million arena with an initial capacity of 15,000 occupied 63 acres of Mitchel Field, a former Army/Air Force base.

1972: The New York Islanders enter the National Hockey League
The Islanders won four consecutive Stanley Cup championships between 1980 and 1983, the seventh of eight dynasties recognized by the NHL in its history.

1973: The Hargrave Vineyard
Louisa and Alex Hargrave planted the first Long Island vineyard, in Cutchogue.

February 5 – 7, 1978: The Long Island Blizzard of 1978
Long Island MacArthur Airport reported 25.9 inches of snow, paralyzing the entire Island. Airports were closed for 48 hours.

September 26 – 28, 1985: Hurricane Gloria
Gloria, a category three storm, was the first major storm to affect Long Island directly since Hurricane Donna in 1960. It made landfall on Long Island, causing beach erosion and mass evacuations. Called the "Storm of the Century" by the media, it caused 683,000 homes and businesses to lose power, including two thirds of all utility customers. Gloria was 300 miles wide with sustained winds of 85 to 100 miles per hour.

1985: Long Island's "Island" Status is questioned
In *United States v. Maine* (1985), the U.S. Supreme Court treated the island as a peninsula for the purpose of a boundary decision. Despite the ruling, the United States Board on Geographic Names considers Long Island an island because it is surrounded by water.

2000: Long Island Ducks baseball team is founded
This professional baseball team is a member of the Liberty Division of the Atlantic League of Professional Baseball. In black, green, and orange uniforms, the team plays home games at their Central Islip ballpark.

Photo courtesy of the U.S. Coast Guard.

August 15, 2003: Long Island blackout
Sixteen million New Yorkers were without electricity for over a day as "the grid" went dark.

October 29, 2012: Superstorm Sandy
Hundreds of thousands of Long Islanders were left without power for weeks in the wake of massive damage from winds and storm surge flooding that took down trees, power lines, and buildings. Superstorm Sandy's post-tropical cyclone was so destructive that it would take years to fully recover from the damage.

December 14, 2020: First COVID-19 Vaccine is given in the United States, New Hyde Park
Sandra Lindsay, the director of critical care nursing at Long Island Jewish Medical Center, received the first vaccine shot in the United States, to battle against the Coronavirus pandemic.

Baldwin Inn Bar, Baldwin

The original Baldwin Inn was built in 1825 by Thomas Baldwin. In 1886, it was destroyed by a fire and was rebuilt. In 1907, it was owned by Henry Hebenstreit. The inn was located at the intersection of two main thoroughfares in the heart of Baldwin's business area. As commerce for shipping goods was eventually taken over by the railroad, inns like the Baldwin lost business. The inn was closed in the 1950s.

TOP: July 4, 1907. The Bar at the Baldwin Inn was owned and run by Henry Hebenstreit with his son, Henry Jr. (shown behind the bar). The popular watering hole is the type of place that the television show *Cheers* pays homage to in its opening credits.

BOTTOM: Interior of Baldwin Inn.

All photos courtesy of the Baldwin Historical Society and Museum.

The Big Duck, Flanders

In 1931, Riverhead duck farmer Martin Maurer built The Duck as a shop to sell ducks and duck eggs. Originally in Riverhead, the Duck "nested" in Flanders, then Hampton Bays, and now finds its permanent home at the Big Duck Ranch in Flanders. Inside is a shop selling "duck architecture" themed items. This ferrocement duck-shaped building is 20 feet tall and 30 feet long, and weighs about 30 tons.

The Big Duck is modeled after the Pekin duck for which Long Island is famous. The duck's eyes are the taillights of a Model T Ford. The Big Duck is *the* iconic Long Island roadside attraction. It was added to the National Register of Historic Places in 1997.

TOP: The Big Duck.
Photo by Shane Levine.

TOP RIGHT: The Big Duck signage.
Photo by Kathleen Balsamo.

LEFT: Posing at the Big Duck.
Photo by Stacy Mandel Kaplan.

Bald Hill, Farmingville

Situated on top of Bald Hill, one of the highest points on Long Island, is the Vietnam Veterans Memorial. It was dedicated on Veteran's Day, November 11, 1991. The monument acknowledges the service and sacrifice of all Vietnam Veterans.

The four-sided 100-foot-high obelisk, emblazoned with the United States flag's red, white and blue stars and stripes, is made of Georgia Cherokee marble and aluminum. Stephen Hayduk Engineering, P.C. of Port Jefferson created the design.

Sign painter, Ed, shared some insight into how this sharply sloping pyramid adorns the bold colors of our nation's flag: "the base of the

ABOVE: Bald Hill Vietnam Veterans Memorial. *Photo by Mike J. Maietta.*

LEFT: The apex of the Bald Hill Vietnam Veterans Memorial. *Photo by Kathleen Balsamo.*

monument is stone, and the flag is painted on aluminum panels adhered to a steel framework that is affixed to the top. I worked as a painter at the sign company that was subcontracted for the job. The first set of panels did not line up, so I was lifted high up in a bucket by a huge crane to precisely measure and mark off for the panel installation. I spray-painted the panels in our shop with the iconic stars and stripes, and they were installed using special cranes that had to reach from the base of the hill to the highest point of the monument."

Privately funded, the Vietnam War Memorial cost approximately $1.3 million to construct. It is located on a 6.5-acre site that is 320 feet above sea level and is open 24 hours a day, seven days a week. From the base, visitors have a view of the Great South Bay, Fire Island and the Atlantic Ocean to the south. To the north, the Long Island Sound and Connecticut can be seen. At night, it is illuminated by floodlights, making it visible from Connecticut.

RIGHT: Bald Hill Ski Bowl. *Photo courtesy of Farmingville Historical Society.*

BELOW: Jayne's Hill sign. *Photo courtesy of Roslyn Landmarks Society.*

Bald Hill Ski Bowl

From January 21, 1965 until it closed in 1980, Bald Hill was the site of a Town-owned ski area known as the Bald Hill Ski Bowl. The Bald Hill Ski Slope was 344 feet tall. The Ski Bowl covered 74 acres located on the northwest part of North Ocean Avenue. It is now known as the Brookhaven Amphitheater, off Bicycle Path.

Bald Hill Ski Bowl was the largest ski area ever to operate on Long Island. It had Long Island's only overhead cable lift, a T-bar, and two rope tows on a vertical drop of 200 feet. Many Long Islanders first learned how to ski there. It closed due to changing weather patterns and a lack of snow, especially after a very mild winter in 1980.

Jayne's Hill, West Hills

Despite popular belief, Bald Hill is not the highest point on Long Island. The highest elevation in the Bald Hill area is 331 feet. The true highest point belongs to the place where Walt Whitman walked, Jayne's Hill, in the town of Huntington, at 401 feet.

Bethpage State Park

Bethpage State Park is a 1,477-acre park on the border of Nassau and Suffolk Counties. It was developed from the Yoakum family estate where the Lenox Hills Country Club was built in the 1930s as part of the Depression Era public-works project, and opened in 1936. Golf course architect A.W. Tillinghast and park superintendent Joseph Burbeck designed three golf courses which they named Black, Red, and Blue. They modified the Lenox Hills Course which became the Green Course. In 1958, Alfred Tull designed the Yellow Course.

TOP: Main building in the 1940s.

ABOVE: Horse and buggy transportation from the Farmingdale Long Island Rail Road (LIRR) Station to Bethpage State Park during World War II.

Bethpage Black Golf Course

The Black Course at Bethpage State Park is a world-renowned 7,468-yard golf course that is one of the most feared and revered courses, public or private, in the United States. It was the site of the U.S. Open in 2002 and 2009, The Barclays in 2012 and 2016, and the PGA Championship in 2019. The Black Course is the most difficult of the five 18-hole regulation golf courses at the park.

For experienced golfers, the famous course is challenging. "Golfers face a 7,468-yard brute that puts every shot and skill to the test," boasts Bethpage State Park of the Black Golf Course. "From the middle tees, it's just short of 6,700 yards, nearly as long or longer than many full-length courses on the Island. The subtle angles and protective cross bunkers present in the layout are characteristics of many celebrated Tillinghast courses." To play a round of golf on the Bethpage Black Course is a desire by golfers on Long Island and around the world.

WARNING
The Black Course Is An Extremely Difficult Course Which We Recommend Only For Highly Skilled Golfers

ABOVE: Bethpage Golfers in the 1940s.

All photos courtesy of Farmingdale-Bethpage Historical Society and the Farmingdale Public Library Digital Photograph Collection.

United States Open Championship – U.S. OPEN 2002

The 102nd U.S. Open was held at the Black Course of the Bethpage State Park from June 13-16, 2002. Tiger Woods was the champion ahead of runner-up Phil Mickelson by three shots. It was the second U.S. Open victory for Woods and the eighth major championship win of his career.

Woods' fame would continue as he achieved a career "grand slam," winning all the major golf tournaments (the U.S. Open, Open Championship, PGA Championship and Masters) within his career. A golfer's grand slam is now also known as the "Tiger Slam."

Past Champion Tiger Woods commented on his 2002 U.S. Open Victory: *"It's awesome to win the nation's title, on a public facility, in front of these fans."*

RIGHT: 2002 Ticket to the U.S. Open.

Bethpage Air Show at Jones Beach State Park

Since 2004, the annual Bethpage Air Show at Jones Beach State Park each Memorial Day weekend marks the traditional start of the Summer season on Long Island. Spectators gaze high above to see air performances by all branches of the U.S. Military. The show often includes the U.S. Navy Blue Angels, the U.S. Air Force Thunderbirds, the U.S. Army Parachute Team the Golden Knights, The U.S. Coast Guard Search and Rescue Demonstration, and Civilian participation by Farmingdale State College Aviation, the American Airpower Museum Warbirds, and others.

More than 200,000 people attend the yearly event. Jones Beach parking lots often fill up by 8:00 am or earlier on the day of the event. Attendees watch from Jones Beach, or from boats on Zach's Bay or the Atlantic Ocean, following Coast Guard restrictions. The event is sponsored by New York State Parks Recreation and Historic Preservation and private local sponsors.

ABOVE: The U.S. Navy flight demonstration squadron, the Blue Angels, performs the Delta Roll at the Bethpage Air Show at Jones Beach. Jones Beach, New York, May 25, 2018.
Photo by Mass Communication Specialist 1st Class Ian Cotter, courtesy of the U.S. Navy.

LEFT: Petty Officer 1st Class Reece Williams from Coast Guard Air Station Cape Cod performs a search and rescue demonstration for more than 200,000 spectators at the Bethpage Air Show, May 25, 2019. Shown in the background is the Jones Beach "Pencil" Water Tower.
Photo by B.A. Van Sise, courtesy of the U.S. Coast Guard.

Frank's Steaks and the Lincoln Inn, Rockville Centre

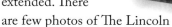

The Lincoln Inn

Part of the original porch was left intact but a portion was removed when the dining-room was extended. There are few photos of The Lincoln Inn, but memories remain strong. It was a celebrated place for parties and business events and families to gather for special occasions. In the 1970s, 1980s, and 1990s, it was known as one of the top restaurants on Long Island's South Shore.

Above image courtesy of Frank's Steaks.
Photo from the 1940s (right) courtesy of the Rockville Centre Historical Society and the Phillips House Museum.

In 1870, a large residential home was constructed for Robert William Hutcheson, M.D. at 54 Lincoln Avenue, Rockville Centre. The property included a spacious horse and carriage barn on 16 acres on the south side of Lincoln Avenue. It took two years for carpenter Matt Robbins to build to the owner's specifications. Each floor had six generous rooms; a kitchen and wash bathroom was off the back, and maids' rooms were in the attic. A covered porch ran the length of the front of the house, and a double front door opened into a front center hall. Dr. Hutcheson was the first Rockville Centre physician. He built a few homes in the area, and sold this home in 1893. It is the only R.W. Hutcheson house that still stands today.

The Hutcheson house was later called Ketcham Lodge. It became a rooming place called the Lincoln Arms Manor, and eventually it was known as The Lincoln Inn.

Frank's Steaks of Rockville Centre

The tradition of fine dining at 54 Lincoln Avenue continues. In October 2002, Frank's Steaks of Rockville Centre opened. Chris Meyer, then a waiter, and now Managing Partner, is the "Face of Frank's Steaks." His desire to create an elite dining experience for everyone is evident in how he treats his staff and in how he warmly welcomes everyone who walks through the doors.

"Having a career that makes people feel like they're at home, surrounded by warm and authentic people, is the goal," Meyer says. "The food and experience speak for themselves."

Frank's Steaks remains a top Long Island restaurant. As you sit in the comfortable dining room and sample the Romanian Skirt Steak (called the "Best Skirt Steak On Earth" by *Zagat Survey*) you become part of the 150-year-history of this iconic location.

The Fashion Industry on Long Island

Long Island's fashion industry has a grand and elegant history. Noted for women's evening wear, including clothing for weddings, high school proms, bar/bat/b'nai mitzvahs and other formal events, Long Island shops and made-to-measure establishments emerged to meet the growing needs of fashion trends. Numerous boutiques and stores carry exclusive designers renowned in the fashion world.

Fashion Boutique Stores

Runway Couture, Bellmore

In 2010, Runway Couture opened to provide special occasion womenswear. Operating like a New York City design house, Runway is owned and operated by fashion designer Kimberly Towers and technical designer Blanca Fuentes. Runway is Long Island's top destination for women's evening, cocktail and special occasion wear.

Runway's custom designs and couture evening wear are internationally acclaimed. Towers' designs have graced the runway at the Louvre in Paris, France. Several custom-made *Kimberly Towers* designs were worn on the Bravo television shows *The Real Housewives of New York* and *The Real Housewives of Miami*.

LEFT: Fashion Designer Kimberly Towers creates sketches for a new dress design.
RIGHT: Runway owners Kim and Blanca. *Photo by Eric Brian Photography, courtesy of Runway Couture.*
BELOW: PM Boutique Store, 1980s. *Photo courtesy of Lila Gaitan.*

PM Boutique LTD, Oceanside

In 1974, Lila Gaitan opened Fashion Hut at the corner of Long Beach Road and Cortland Avenue in Oceanside. Gaitan was a custom designer who sold her own designs, as well as beautiful ready-to-wear outfits. After a vehicle accident involving a gas truck and a car, the Fashion Hut location was destroyed.

In 1981, Gaitan partnered with Rosalie Silber, an expert in fashion buying and marketing. They launched P.M. Boutique Ltd., The Fashion Hut, in Lincoln Plaza in Oceanside. Gaitan ran the technical end and alterations and Silber handled buying, merchandising and sales. From the 1980s through the 2000s, it was the Long Island go-to store for women's evening wear fashions. The business was sold in 2010, and closed in 2013.

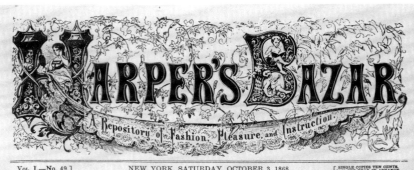

Harper's Bazaar

Mary Louise Booth was born in Millville (now Yaphank) on April 19, 1831. In 1867, Booth served as Editor-in-Chief of the first women's fashion magazine, *Harper's Bazaar,* which was a weekly publication at that time. It was the style resource for "women who are the first to buy the best, from casual to couture." The magazine publishes monthly issues highlighting couture and accessible fashion trends. In July, 2020, the magazine named a new Editor-in-Chief, Samira Nasr, who is the first person of color to lead the magazine in its history.

Famous Fashion Designers from Long Island

Michael David Kors was born on August 9, 1959. Born Karl Anderson Jr., Kors grew up in Merrick and graduated from John F. Kennedy High School in Bellmore. In 1981, he launched his Michael Kors women's label at New York City's Bergdorf Goodman store. In 2004, the Michael Kors line MICHAEL was launched, adding to the Michael Kors Collection label.

Kenneth Cole was born on March 23, 1954, in Brooklyn, and graduated from the John L. Miller Great Neck North High School in 1972. In 1982, he founded fashion house Kenneth Cole Productions. Kenneth Cole designs men's and women's footwear and clothing.

Donna Karan was born Donna Ivy Faske on October 2, 1948. She lived in Woodmere in the Five Towns and graduated from Hewlett High School in 1966. She is known for her Donna Karan New York and DKNY clothing brand, as well as for her lifestyle brand, Urban Zen.

Fashion Trends on Long Island

In the 1940s during WWII, American patriotism influenced fashion. Clothing featured red, white, and blue colors. Women wore natural makeup with bright red lips. As men left for war, a national campaign recruited females to the workforce. American women entered the workplace up 63 percent from pre-war years, especially in the areas of munitions and aircraft, in locations such as the Grumman Corp. in Bethpage.

Women wore masculine clothing, including trousers and overalls. Rosie the Riveter became a cultural icon as the epitome of the overall-clad, female factory worker. As the decade progressed, dresses became shorter, and women's two-piece outfits became popular. Men wore suits, while women wore modest dresses. Peep-toe shoes, wedge sandals, and loafers were the fashionable women's footwear.

In the 1947 post-war era, designer Christian Dior introduced dresses with an hourglass silhouette. Women wore slimmer skirts with a pinched "roaming" waistline that stayed popular throughout the 1950s. Men wore three-piece suits with vests of contrasting colors. Casual men's clothing included patterned jackets, khakis, slacks, and cardigans. A street look of grease-slicked hair, leather jackets, dungaree jeans, and converse sneakers contrasted the conventional, prep school look of blazers, polo shirts, and sweater vests.

1947. Shoulder pads and masculine details were popular. Shockingly, women even wore pants. A man looked dapper in his double-breasted suit.
Photo courtesy of Katharine Nesemann Bruzzo.

1940s. The tailored look prevailed and creating polished chic was an art. Hats were worn for day and evening. A hat with coque feathers meant a serious occasion. Peep-toe shoes, pearls, gloves and matching purse showed elegance and refinement. And, a lady never forgot her red lips.
Photo courtesy of Katharine Nesemann Bruzzo.

Women's fashion in the 1960s was heavily influenced by the media. First Lady Jackie Kennedy Onassis, born in Southampton and raised in East Hampton and Manhattan, wore tailored suit-dresses that trended. Men neglected the classic, gray three-piece suit and replaced it with button down shirts, turtle necks, and knit sweaters. The "Mod(ern) style," consisting of mini skirts, trousers, and boots, dominated the fashion world. Hippie fashion was inspired by a Bohemian lifestyle, and included bell-bottom jeans, flowing caftans, and tie-dyed clothing with vivid designs.

ABOVE: 1960s. Jackie Kennedy and Audrey Hepburn inspired this 1965 Oceanside High School May Queen Beauty Pageant winner, who chose a pleated, tea-length dress with a bateau neckline, a pearl necklace, elbow-length gloves, and an updo. *Photo courtesy of Kathy Bruzzo Towers.*

BELOW: 1965. Six high school girls going out to dinner at Sunrise Village, Bellmore, to celebrate a birthday. Note the frosted eyeshadow and beehive hairdo.
Photo courtesy of Kathy Bruzzo Towers.

RIGHT: 1980s. This turquoise taffeta bridesmaid gown exemplified the decade's motto: the bigger the better, with oversized puff sleeves, peplums, and rich, bright colors. Even the hair was big, thanks to jumbo rollers, curling irons, and teasing.
Photo courtesy of Daurene Lanning.

The 1970s introduced casual, gender-neutral clothing of bold colors and patterns. Men's suits were made with pastel colors, plaid, and denim. The latest dance craze, disco, peaked in the mid-1970s as portrayed in the 1977 movie *Saturday Night Fever*. The flamboyant dance style introduced women's evening outfits with glitter and sequins. Chunky heels transitioned to strappy sandals. To appear taller and create the illusion of an elongated body, men wore tight-fitting shirts, wide belts, and turtlenecks.

What followed was a decade of big hair and bright colors. Fashion trends in the early 1980s were influenced by broadcasts from Manhattan's MTV Studios. Women's hair featured teased volume, crimps, and curls. Earrings were large and dramatic. Women wore fitted and high-waisted jeans, shoulder pads, and cut-neck sweatshirts. A new aerobics fitness movement popularized leotards, spandex fabric, and leg warmers. Accessories such as fanny packs, scrunchies and fingerless gloves were worn. Men wore sweaters, polo shirts, and suspenders. In the late 1980s, singer/songwriter Debbie Gibson from Merrick influenced a popular look of hats and short denim jackets. Sneaker brands such as Adidas, Reebok, and Air Jordan were fashionable, vastly different from the heels and wedges of the past.

Carol Silva

Carol Silva is a veteran, Emmy Award-winning news anchor from News 12 Long Island. In March 1987, Carol began sharing Long Island life from the anchor desk of the world's first 24-hour regional news network. During her 33 years there, she also reported live from Ground Zero after 9/11 in New York City, and traveled across the country covering State and Congressional hearings and Presidential elections.

Carol was born in St. Albans Naval Hospital in Queens in 1954. Her father had served there during part of his 20 years as a Naval Corpsman with the First Marine Division, but he was often stationed far from home. Carol and her brothers grew up in a Levitt home in a Hicksville neighborhood filled with other kids of WWII veterans.

In 1963, Carol's father retired from the military. After family dinners, he joined other neighborhood dads walking house-to-house with donation coin cans, to raise money to help build affordable Catholic Diocesan high schools including Holy Trinity High School. Carol graduated from that very same school in 1972.

Carol attended Nassau Community College in Garden City and the University of Dayton in Ohio, but got her start in news at New York Institute of Technology (NYIT), in Old Westbury. The final project in Carol's Introduction to Radio class required her to write, produce and deliver a 15-minute radio show, including a five-minute newscast. Her professor took her tape to WBAB radio in Babylon where he was a DJ, and she was subsequently hired as weekend News Anchor. Carol moved from WBAB to other stations including WGBB in Merrick and WLIR/WDRE in Hempstead.

Carol has earned more than 40 journalism awards including three Emmys. In 2018, NYIT awarded her an Honorary Doctorate degree. In 2019, she was inducted into the prestigious Silver Circle of the New York Chapter of the National Academy of Television, Arts & Sciences and into the Long Island Journalism Hall of Fame. Carol is also a New York State "Woman of Distinction." A Mexican American, Carol was proudly named Hispanic of the Year by the Suffolk County Police Department and a Hispanic role model by the Nassau County Hispanic Cultural Association.

"Studio 14 in 1983." Cable television founder, Charles Dolan, had created the first online television guide on Cablevision's Channel 14. He believed 37 television channels could overwhelm viewers who had been used to a choice of only 13 channels. Carol Silva was a live, nighttime Studio 14 anchor, explaining the nightly programming choices available on each channel. To this day, updated versions of Mr. Dolan's alphanumeric channels still tell viewers where to access their programs.

In June 2019, Carol announced that in December of that year she would wrap up her 44-year career and retire as News 12 Morning Show Anchor. On September 16, 2019, Carol led the Executive Leadership panel for the international WICT Leadership Conference (Women in Cable Telecommunications) in New York City. Two days later, she went back to her doctor due to a persistent cough. On September 26, 2019, Carol was diagnosed with Stage 4 cancer. A golf-ball sized tumor in her left lung had spread to 12 additional tumors in her brain. The oncologist's devastating news was met with silence by Carol and her husband and best friend. Even Carol herself was surprised by the next words that she spoke.

"Thank you, God, for my healing."

Her doctors at Northwell's Monter Cancer Center in New Hyde Park predicted that her hopeful attitude would help her. Fifty weeks later, Carol was cancer-free.

Carol lives on Long Island with her husband, Bob. They have three grown children, Jason, Connor and Shane. Carol does motivational speaking, focusing on finding your power and coming back from defeat. She often shows off her 1983 Cablevision rejection letter that she proudly displayed in every Cablevision office she occupied.

Carol Silva says everyone has a story. She began her next chapter in 2022 with her podcast, *The Silva Lining*. It focuses on those moments most of us have suffered, when we fear a setback has ruined our chances in life. Carol and her guests explore how so often those experiences knock us in the right direction; and that is – *The Silva Lining*.

TOP RIGHT: December 2, 2019. Carol Silva standing in front of the *News 12 Long Island* anchor desk the morning she returned from two months of treatments for stage 4 cancer.

BOTTOM RIGHT: 2010. Just another morning of typical shenanigans for the people Carol calls "The family I choose." Shown is Carol's *News 12 Long Island* Morning team family: Elisa DiStefano, entertainment and traffic reporter; Carol Silva; Elizabeth Hashagen, co-anchor; and Meteorologist Rich Hoffman. *Photos courtesy of Carol Silva.*

News 12 Long Island

On December 15, 1986, *News 12 Long Island* was launched by Cablevision from Woodbury. It was the first 24-hour regional cable news service in the United States. Since 2016, it has been owned by Altice USA. It had been previously owned by Newsday Media Holdings. News 12 was exclusively available on Cable Television until November 4, 2019, when Verizon FiOS began to carry News 12. When she retired in 2020, News 12 renamed its studio, the "Carol Silva Studio" to honor Silva's distinguished career.

Greenport

In the mid-1600s, colonists from New Haven, Connecticut crossed the Long Island Sound and settled in the North Fork of Long Island in the township of Southold, which includes what is now the Village of Greenport. Greenport has been known by several different names including Winter Harbor, Stirling, and Green Hill. In 1831, the name Greenport was adopted. Greenport was officially established in 1838, and was the First Incorporated Village in the State of New York.

The fishing and boating industries grew strong in Greenport. Greenport was a major whaling port and shipbuilding industrial site between 1795 and 1859. In the mid-1800s, the fishing industry was a major source of employment. The arrival of the Long Island Rail Road in 1844 caused the development of Greenport as local farmers used the railroad to ship their harvest to markets. In the early 20th century, Greenport was a huge oystering center. Today, it remains a hub for marine and boating, fishing, and for its vineyards. *Photo by Scott J. Mandel.*

RIGHT: Greenport fishing boats, 1955.
Photo by Max Henry Hubacher, courtesy of the New York Public Library.

Greenport's deep and protected harbor along Gardiner's Bay fostered the development of the fishing industry in this Long Island village. Singer/songwriter Billy Joel pays tribute to this part of Long Island and to Long Island's struggling fishing industry and to the fishermen/baymen, in his 1989 song *The Downeaster 'Alexa'*, from Joel's Grammy-nominated *Storm Front* album, with lyrics such as: "We took on diesel back in Montauk yesterday, And left this morning from the bell in Gardiner's Bay..."

The song speaks to the challenges and hard work of the Oyster Bay fishermen. The 'Alexa' was a boat Billy Joel had owned, named after his daughter, Alexa Ray Joel. Joel worked on an oyster boat on Long Island in his youth.

The Greenport Jail

In June, 1917, the Greenport Village Jail was completed. It is a brick and cement fireproof building, with three steel cells. The basement has a sleeping room with bunks for traveling salesmen and hobos. It was constructed by D. Stanley Corwin (1875-1938) who also built the Greenport Public Library and the Greenport Theatre. The jail was used until 1995, when the Greenport Police Department was disbanded and exists today as the Greenport Jail and Police Museum site.

Photo by Scott J. Mandel.

Greenport's Old Kindergarten Schoolhouse

Built in 1818, this small, one-room schoolhouse was located on North Road. Children from Arshamomaque, Stirling (now Greenport) and East Marion attended there until 1832, when a larger schoolhouse was built. In 1879, the first kindergarten was established and the old schoolhouse was moved to 4th Avenue and South Street. Greenport kindergarten students attended until 1932. It was closed for decades and in 2005 moved to First and Front Streets. In 2010, the schoolhouse building was renovated and restored. Today it is the village's first historic and interpretive center and is utilized for community meetings and events.

Photos by Scott J. Mandel.

The Jess Owen Carousel House

The Jess Owen Carousel House is an antique carousel located in Mitchell Park, Greenport. It was built in 1920 by the Herschell-Spillman Company in North Tonawanda, New York (near Buffalo) who made wooden carousels propelled by steam boilers. From 1920 to the 1950s, the carousel was part of a traveling carnival, and was then located at a farmer's market in Nassau County. In 1955, The Grumman Company acquired the carousel for use at company picnics at their Calverton plant. After Northrop Grumman Corporation closed its Calverton location in 1996, the carousel was boarded up in a pavilion. Greenport Village Mayor David Kapell, the Village Board and local civic associations campaigned and the Northrop Grumman Carousel was moved to Greenport in 1997. It was re-named for Jess Owen, the carousel's caretaker prior to it being relocated to Greenport.

During the "Golden Age of Carousels," from 1880 to 1930, over 5,000 wooden carousels were carved. The Jess Owen Carousel House in Greenport is one of fewer than 180 wooden carousels that remain in the United States today.

Joey Kola

Joey Kola was born on October 19, 1961, in Williamsburg, Brooklyn. Like so many Long Islanders, his family moved eastward when he was a baby. He grew up in East Bay Shore and attended Islip High School. Kola attended Suffolk Community College in Brentwood, where he studied theater, and C.W. Post (later called Long Island University LIU Post) in Brookville, where he graduated with a degree in Business. Throughout the course of his studies, he was performing at local comedy clubs, such as Richie Minervini's East Side Comedy Club in Huntington, and Governor's Comedy Club in Levittown. He worked with comedians such as Bob Nelson, Rosie O'Donnell, and Kevin James.

Kola cultivated his skills as an entertainer when he was young, learning from his relatives who either sang or told jokes at family gatherings. He credits his parents, aunts, and uncles for encouraging him to perform.

Married since 1987, his wife and childhood sweetheart, Leanora, is his greatest inspiration. His kids, family life, pets, suburbia, and domestication are all fodder for his act. Not only has he been a stand-up comedian for over four

Joey Kola rockin' a Saturday night full house at Governors in Levittown. *Photo by John Blenn. Matchbook photo courtesy of Caroline Pisaniello.*

decades, he has been a TV Warm Up Comedian for television studio audiences since 1993. He was voted the Best TV Warm Up Comedian in New York City by *Time Out Magazine*. Some of his television warm up credits include audiences for Rosie O'Donnell, Jon Stewart, Martha Stewart, *America's Got Talent*, Rachael Ray, and Drew Barrymore.

Joey Kola is still one of the funniest comics performing at Long Island comedy clubs, as well as theaters and clubs around the country and abroad. Kola's high energy, spot-on punchlines, and topical and timeless material are legendary to his audiences everywhere, especially to his home crowd on Long Island.

The Pencil, The Jones Beach Water Tower

As you drive south towards the Atlantic Ocean, where the Wantagh State Parkway and Ocean Parkway meet, is a landscaped traffic circle. At the center is "The Pencil."

Throughout the decades, visitors posed for photos at the Jones Beach Water Tower. It serves as the iconic symbol that you have arrived at the Long Island destination of Jones Beach.

Built in 1930, The Pencil is 231 feet tall, and extends more than 1,000 feet underground. Robert Moses, president of the Long Island State Parks Commission, supervised the construction. The tower is made of Ohio sandstone and Barbizon brick. The point is made of copper and is 32 feet high. The architectural design was inspired by the Venice, Italy bell tower of St. Mark's Basilica.

The Pencil is a functioning water tower holding 315,000 gallons of water. It supplies fresh water to the entire park, including the Jones Beach Theater, swimming pools, restrooms, and bathhouses.

RIGHT: *Jones Beach Water Tower,* watercolor painting by artist Michael White. White shares his vision of "The Pencil" and his childhood memory that the sight of the tower in the distance on Ocean Parkway meant that the beach day had started. The imagery of the cloud above is shaped like a map of Long Island, and the Pencil is pointing to itself on the "map." *Photo courtesy of Michael White.*

BELOW: Jones Beach visitors, July 8, 1951.
Photo courtesy of Denise Fussell.

Jones Beach Theater

Summers on Long Island include the outdoor concert series at The Jones Beach Marine Theater, an outdoor amphitheater located on Zach's Bay, a half mile north of the beach. It is the go-to spot to see famous musicians perform during the summer months.

The theater as it stands now opened June 26, 1952. It replaced a wooden structure that was the Jones Beach Marine Stadium of the 1930s that had been demolished in 1945. An artificial island was created with dredged sand to develop the space. The 8,200-seat theatre had a moat — a water gap separating the seating and the stage. An underwater tunnel connected the main theatre to the stage. Performers used the tunnel or were brought to the stage by motor boat. Guy Lombardo would arrive by boat and take his place in front of his orchestra. The cost to build the theater was $4 million (which would be $43.5 million in 2020 dollars).

The Theater has had many names over the decades: New Jones Beach Marine Stadium (1952–53), Jones Beach Marine Theater (1954–1994), Jones Beach Amphitheater (1994–2000), Jones Beach Theater (2000–2002), Tommy Hilfiger at Jones Beach Theater (2002–2006), Nikon at Jones Beach Theater (2006–2016), and Northwell Health at Jones Beach Theater (2017–present).

Musicals were the main attraction until the 1980s when it became a concert venue. A 1991 renovation added a second level (and filled in the moat) and increased seating to 11,200, and a second expansion in 1998 rose to 15,000 seats. Jimmy Buffett is a frequent performer at the theater and has played the venue over 30 times.

Concerts go on rain or shine, unless there is lightning. Any frequent Jones Beach concert goer comes prepared with a rain jacket, and will share stories of seeing their favorite artist performing in the summer rain.

OPPOSITE PAGE BOTTOM: Nick Carter at the Tommy Hilfiger at Jones Beach Theater.

OPPOSITE PAGE: David Bowie performing at Jones Beach Theater in the rain.

Photos by and courtesy of celebrity/rock photographer, Long Island's Kevin Mazur.

LEFT: Jones Beach Marine Theater in the 1950s, where a water moat divided the seating and the theater stage. *Photo by C. Manley DeBevoise, courtesy of the New York Public Library.*

BELOW: Jones Beach bicyclist outside the Nikon at Jones Beach Theater. *Photo by Denise Rafkind.*

Jones Beach State Park,
Wantagh

Jones Beach is a summer destination that was created in 1929. The 6.5-mile-long park along the Atlantic Ocean was named for Major Thomas Jones, who created a whaling station on the outer part of Jones Beach. It is the largest public recreational bathing park in the world, and is unmatched as one of the world's most magnificent beaches.

On August 4, 1929, as part of the New York State Park System, Jones Beach was dedicated by Governor Franklin D. Roosevelt, and the nautical vision of Commission President Robert Moses.

Three parkways link Jones Beach: Ocean Parkway, Wantagh State Parkway, and Meadowbrook State Parkway. The Meadowbrook Parkway was originally established as a right of way for an additional causeway from the mainland, near Freeport, to the Park. "The Pencil" Water Tower stands tall at the spot where the parkways meet.

Top attractions at the Park throughout the decades have been swimming (in the Atlantic Ocean, as well as in swimming pools with diving and wading pools), surfing, volleyball, deck tennis and shuffleboard, golf courses, miniature golf, basketball, and softball.

TOP LEFT: Boat on the beach near the Atlantic Ocean. *Photo courtesy of the U.S. Coast Guard.*

TOP RIGHT: Postcard from the 1930s, boardwalk, beach, and the ocean.

CENTER RIGHT: Postcard from the 1950s, watertower and beach.

BOTTOM RIGHT: Seahorse banner from the 1950s.

There is also a children's playground, picnic areas, bird watching, miles of surf fishing areas, fishing docks, a boat basin, and a two-mile-long boardwalk. Jones Beach is renowned for its annual events that include an Air Show, Fireworks Spectacular, Concerts, Sports programs, and outdoor entertainment.

Jovia Financial Credit Union

LEFT: Original location of Valley Stream Teachers Federal Credit Union in Valley Stream, 1938.

BELOW: Staff outside the Valley Stream Teachers Federal Credit Union. *Photos courtesy of Jovia Financial Credit Union.*

BOTTOM: Jovia Financial Credit Union, Valley Stream, 2021.
Photo by Rishe Poonai.

In 1938, the Valley Stream Teachers Federal Credit Union was founded to serve local teachers of Valley Stream, Long Island. In 1981, the credit union expanded to service teachers and their families under the name Nassau Educators Federal Credit Union, and officially changed its name to NEFCU in 2006. On September 23, 2019, it re-branded as Jovia Financial Credit Union.

President and CEO, John Deieso, explained, "... we needed a new name; one that connects us to all of Long Island and Long Islanders." Jovia (JO-vee-ah), derived from the word jovial, connotes optimism, trust, and "banking on the bright side." Over 200,000 Long Islanders rely daily on the 21 branches that stretch across Long Island from the New York City border to central Suffolk County. "I am so proud that Jovia plays a role in Long Island's rich history. As a lifelong Long Islander, nothing makes me happier than supporting and lifting our residents and communities, as we've been doing for over 80 years." says Deieso.

The credit union's educator roots remain deep, as it supports and promotes education with scholarships, teacher grants and financial literacy programs. For many growing up on Long Island, the credit union was the source of funding for their very first car loan, or their first childhood savings account.

Charles Lindbergh's Historic Flight

Long Island is the birthplace of international air travel. On May 20, 1927, Charles Lindbergh, in his airplane *Spirit of St. Louis*, lifted off from Roosevelt Field in Garden City and flew 3,600 miles to Paris, successfully completing the first transatlantic flight in 33 hours. This first non-stop flight from the United States to France would be the start of future international air travel to Europe.

LEFT: Captain Charles Lindbergh and his monoplane that made the non-stop flight from New York to Paris. May 21, 1927. *Photo courtesy of the Baldwin Historical Society and Museum.*

ABOVE: Charles Lindbergh addressing the crowd at a welcome home celebration at Roosevelt Field. 1927. *Photo courtesy of the Cradle of Aviation Museum.*

LINDBERGH'S FLIGHT
ON MAY 20, 1927, COL. CHARLES A. LINDBERGH ROSE ½ MILE WEST FROM ROOSEVELT FIELD, LANDING 33 HOURS LATER AT LE BOURGET FIELD, FRANCE.
STATE EDUCATION DEPARTMENT 1936

Photo by Denise Rafkind.

Airfields and Airports

The airfields of this aviation center have had many names, including the Hempstead Plains Aerodrome, the Hempstead Plains Field, and the Garden City Aerodrome. During World War I, it operated as a training field for the Air Service, United States Army. It was called Hazelhurst Field, named for Lt. Leighton Wilson Hazelhurst Jr. who had died in military service.

On July 16, 1918, it was renamed Mitchel Field, to commemorate John Purroy Mitchel, the former Mayor of New York City who was killed in a flying accident on July 6, 1918, while training with the U.S. Air Service. On September 24, 1918, the Army renamed the eastern portion as Roosevelt Field, to honor President Theodore Roosevelt's son, Quentin, who was killed in air combat during World War I.

The airport fields were purchased in 1929 by Roosevelt Field, Inc., and in the 1930s it was the busiest civilian airfield in the United States. Part of the land was sold in 1936 and became the Roosevelt Raceway. The remainder continued to operate as an aviation center under the name Roosevelt Field. Both Roosevelt Field and Mitchel Field served military functions during World War II.

Photos courtesy of the Baldwin Historical Society and Museum.

LEFT: Roosevelt Field, circa 1935, looking north. Old Country Road runs left to right with Clinton/Glen Cove Road on the left side. During the 1930s Long Island's Roosevelt Field was the busiest and most famous civil airport in the world.

Photo courtesy of the Cradle of Aviation Museum.

On July 1, 1948, Idlewild Airport, an international airport with six runways, opened just 10 miles away in Jamaica, Queens. Idlewild had been the name of the golf club that the airport displaced. On December 24, 1963, the airport was renamed John F. Kennedy International Airport (JFK), just over one month after the assassination of President John F. Kennedy.

The Roosevelt Field Airport closed on May 31, 1951. Long Island's large retail shopping destinations emerged in this location. The original flying field area became the Roosevelt Field Shopping Mall. In 1997, the eastern field area became the Mall at The Source, where Fortunoff was the anchor store.

In 1961, Mitchel Field was decommissioned. It became a complex that now includes the Cradle of Aviation Museum, Nassau Community College and Hofstra University. As one of the first air bases of the United States, The Mitchel Air Base and Flight Line (Charles Lindbergh Boulevard, Ellington Avenue, East and West Roads) were designated on the National Register of Historic Places on May 4, 2018.

ABOVE: Roosevelt Field flightline, circa 1935, looking south. The site of numerous historic flights, including Lindbergh's takeoff, Roosevelt Field was a popular weekend entertainment destination for Long Islanders in the 1920s and 1930s. Air shows were held every weekend.

Roosevelt Field, circa 1950, looking west. The famed airfield closed in 1951 and the mall bearing its name opened in 1957. Old Country Road runs along the right side of the photo. The large hangers lining the road were demolished in 1972.

Photos courtesy of the Cradle of Aviation Museum.

BELOW: Idlewild Airport/New York International, now John F. Kennedy Airport, 1951. Seeing the need for a much larger airport for New York than LaGuardia, the Port Authority built and opened New York International airport (Idlewild) on Jamaica Bay in 1948. Since its inception, the airport has undergone constant expansion and redevelopment, and will likely see further improvements as the demand for air travel continues.

ABOVE: Open House at Mitchel Field, 1954. Historic Mitchel Field, which was founded in 1918, was a major U.S. Army Air Corps base and later an Air Force base until its closing in 1961. The field's annual open house, at which the latest Air Force aircraft were shown, was an immensely popular event.

LEFT: Symbols of the "Jet Age" at Idlewild New York International Airport, 1958. A new Pan American Boeing 707 sits in front of the "new" International Arrivals Building and Control Tower. This building also had a popular rooftop observation deck where visitors, for a dime, could watch the exciting airport action.

All photos courtesy of The Cradle of Aviation Museum.

Cradle of Aviation

LEFT: The NASA Astronaut Statute at The Cradle of Aviation, located where Mitchel Field once stood. The Cradle of Aviation chronicles the contributions of Long Islanders as flyers, designers and builders of air and space craft. The museum preserves a rich aerospace heritage, from early aviation flights in 1909 from Hempstead Plains in a biplane, to man's first steps on the Moon. The Museum and Education Center itself is a cherished location for Long Islanders to visit.

Long Island was a center for the development of aviation. In 1896, the first recorded aircraft flight took place on Long Island. A Lilienthal-type glider was flown from the bluffs along Nassau County's north shore. Long Island's geographic location at the eastern edge of the United States along the Atlantic Ocean, adjacent to the populous New York City, combined with its flat, open landscape, made it a natural airfield. By 1910, three airfields operated on the Hempstead Plains (which would later be Mitchel Field). Flying schools and aircraft factories opened. In 1911, Cal Rodger, in a Wright biplane, flew the first transcontinental flight from Long Island to California in 49 days. In 1927, Charles Lindbergh flew his monoplane from Garden City to Paris, France, in the first transatlantic flight. Due to the seminal flights from Long Island, by the mid-to-late 1920s the cluster of airfields on Long Island was dubbed the "Cradle of Aviation."

ABOVE: The Cradle of Aviation in Garden City is home to the rescued and restored Nunley's Carousel.
Photos by Denise Rafkind.

Roosevelt Field Shopping Mall

Roosevelt Field Shopping Mall in Garden City opened in April, 1955. It was designed by architect I. M. Pei as a single-level, open-air center. The original anchor of the mall was a two-level, 343,000-square-foot Macy's that opened on August 22, 1956. The mall included F.W. Woolworth 5 & 10 store, Walgreens Drug, Food Fair supermarket, Buster Brown Shoes, a public auditorium, a movie theater, and an outdoor ice rink. Over time, other anchor stores included Gimbels (succeeded by Stern's), A&S, and Alexander's (succeeded by Bloomingdale's). Today, the mall has 243 stores with anchor stores of Bloomingdale's, JCPenney, Macy's, Nordstrom, Dick's Sporting Goods, and Neiman Marcus. It is the largest shopping mall on Long Island, the second largest shopping mall in the state of New York, and the eighth largest shopping mall in the United States.

TOP: Aerial view of Roosevelt Field Mall looking south toward Mitchel Field, Roosevelt Raceway on left, Clinton Road on right, 1956.

TOP RIGHT: Roosevelt Field open-air shopping mall, 1957.

BOTTOM RIGHT: Aerial view of the Roosevelt Field Shopping Mall looking south, 1976.

All photos courtesy of the Cradle of Aviation Museum.

Ninedays

LEFT: Ninedays performing at the Paramount in Huntington, 2013. *Photo by Heather Friedfertig Photography.*

ABOVE: Nick, John, Brian, Jeremy, and Vincent at Deepwells Mansion in St. James. *Photo by Neil Tandy.*

Photos courtesy of Ninedays.

The band Ninedays is best known for its May, 2000 mainstream debut album, *The Madding Crowd*, with the hit single "Absolutely (Story of a Girl)," that reached number one on the Billboard Hot 100 chart in the United States. The band was named in 1995, when they recorded their first album, *Something to Listen To*, in just nine days. In 1996 they released their second album, *Monday Songs*.

The Ninedays band members all met through the Long Island music scene, each having a reputation as one of the best musicians in their respective high schools. John Hampson, lead vocals and guitars, graduated from Riverhead High School. Brian Desveaux, lead vocals and guitars, graduated from Centereach High School. Jeremy Dean, keyboards, saxophone, and backing vocals, graduated from Patchogue Medford High School. Nick Dimichino, bass guitar and backing vocals, graduated from Smithtown East High School. Vincent Tattanelli, drums and percussion, graduated from Sachem High School.

They had each played in local bands, and together they played in the cover band Wonderama, performing past and current hits as well as some Ninedays originals. A favorite then was a tune called "Mexico" that was from their third independent release in 1996-97, aptly called *Ninedays Three*. The group played weekly on Mondays at the Village Pub in Port Jefferson. They also frequented the Dublin Pub in Patchogue, Mulcahey's in Wantagh, and the Paramount in Huntington. Ninedays has released seven albums. The most recent was *Snapshots* in 2016.

Hope Sculpture, Centerport

Since 2009, Artist Roberto Julio Bessin's 22-foot-tall, 1,200-pound sculpture of a blue heron looking skyward has been perched in Heron Park in Centerport. The Centerport Harbor Civic Association maintains and preserves the outdoor statue made of welded bronze rods.

The great blue heron is a bird indigenous to New York State. According to North American Native tradition, the blue heron brings messages of self-determination and self-reliance. *Photo by Denise Rafkind.*

Huntington Town House, Huntington

The Town House featured three ballrooms, each with its own kitchen and bandstand. It hosted between 12 to 22 banquets each week and expanded to increase the seating capacity from 900 to 1500 people. By 1972, the Town House had expanded to 11 rooms; and by 2000 it boasted 100,000 square feet of banquet space and parking for 2000 cars on a 20-acre site.

In 1997, the Town House was purchased from Thomas Manno's estate for $7.6 million. In July, 2011, the Huntington Town House catering hall was demolished.

Photo courtesy of Kathy Krieger.

The Huntington Town House was one of the largest catering hall facilities in the United States. For decades, it was Long Island's go-to place for weddings, proms, other celebrations, and events.

Leo Gerard and his father, William B. Gerard, had successes in the hospitality industry. In 1932, Leo leased a restaurant in Cold Spring Harbor under the name The Oyster Bar. It was also called Ye Olde Tavern Inn, or Leo Gerard's. In March, 1937, Gerard purchased a wooded, five-acre estate on the south side of Jericho Turnpike, just east of the Huntington-Amityville Road (Route 110). The property included a large house with a huge dining room that could seat over 100 people. Gerard's restaurant was relocated to the new property and opened three months later.

In 1957, Gerard sold the restaurant to New York caterer, Thomas Manno, who converted it into a catering facility. It was the first facility to be used exclusively for catering on Long Island. Manno named it the Huntington Town House and refurbished the building. With its picturesque country club atmosphere, the Town House was advertised as the perfect venue for wedding receptions.

Long Island Rail Road – The LIRR

The Long Island Rail Road was chartered on April 24, 1834, and has operated continuously ever since. Referred to as the LIRR, it is the oldest railroad in the United States still operating under its original charter and name.

The LIRR was privately owned until the 1960s when it was purchased by the State of New York. It is one of the few services that operates around the clock all year long. The LIRR network runs from the center of Manhattan to eastern Suffolk County, connecting 124 stations along 700 miles of track.

Originally built to reach sparsely populated Long Island, the railways to the south shore (Long Beach), along the north shore (Port Washington), and stretching eastward, helped Long Island to grow in population, and also provided daily transportation to and from New York City and to other parts of Long Island. Over 81 million commuters use the LIRR each year.

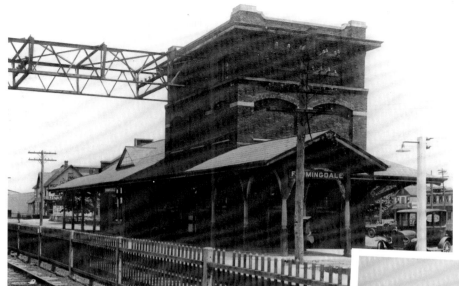

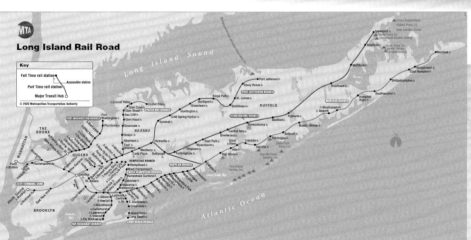

LEFT: Long Beach LIRR Train Station.
Photo courtesy of The Long Beach Historical and Preservation Society.

TOP: Farmingdale Train Station, 1922.
Photo courtesy of Farmingdale-Bethpage Historical Society and the Farmingdale Public Library Digital Photograph Collection.

RIGHT: Long Island Rail Road train near Brentwood, 1945.
Photo by Max Henry Hubacher, courtesy of the New York Public Library.

You will often hear people recite all the stops of a train schedule by heart, such as the 15 stops of the LIRR Babylon line: "This is the train to Babylon, making all stops – NY Penn Station, Jamaica, Rockville Centre, Baldwin, Freeport, Merrick, Bellmore, Wantagh, Seaford, Massapequa, Massapequa Park, Amityville, Copiague, Lindenhurst, and Babylon," and if you need to "change at Jamaica" for other destinations.

Montauk Point Lighthouse

Out at the tip of eastern Long Island is the oldest lighthouse in New York State, the Montauk Point Lighthouse. It is one of twenty lighthouses on Long Island that aid in navigation to keep waterways safe.

From the top of the lighthouse is a spectacular view of Block Island Sound, the Atlantic Ocean, and beyond.

The lighthouse was authorized under President George Washington, and construction was completed on November 5, 1792. It was designated as a National Historic Landmark on March 5, 2012.

TOP: Mom and daughter posing at Montauk Point, 1970s.
Photo courtesy of Carolyn Briggs-Leavitt.

LEFT: *Photo by Kathleen Balsamo.*

Muttontown Preserve, Muttontown

The Muttontown Preserve is Nassau County's largest nature preserve at 550 acres. It was created as a combination of three former estates: The Knollwood Estate, The Chelsea Mansion, and Nassau Hall. Knollwood only exists today as ruins. The other two existing mansions stand today and represent Long Island's Gold Coast Era.

LEFT: Shown here are the ruins of the Knollwood Estate, which had been a 60-room granite mansion designed by architects Hiss and Weekes. King Zog, the last monarch of Albania, acquired the property in 1951 to build a new palace. Zog never lived there and instead sold the estate in 1955 to Lansdell Christie. Rumors circulated about hidden treasures within the mansion walls, attracting vandals and looters to the abandoned property. The Christies had the mansion demolished in 1959, but evidence of it lingers as ruins of stairs and broken fountains. *Photo courtesy of Bill Barash.*

TOP: The Chelsea Mansion was built in 1924, and its architecture contained French, English and Chinese influences. It was owned by Alexandra Emery Moore and her husband, Benjamin Moore. (Benjamin was the great, great grandson of Clement Clarke Moore, author of the poem "A Visit from St. Nicholas," better known as "T'was the Night Before Christmas.") Chelsea was named for the New York City area where Mr. Moore's ancestors had lived for generations. Mr. Moore gave the Village of Muttontown its name and served as its first mayor from 1931 to 1938.

BOTTOM: Nassau Hall was built in 1903, and was modeled after Mount Vernon, the first home of President George Washington. Nassau Hall was built by architects Delano & Aldrich for Frederic Bronson Winthrop. It was known originally as the Egerton L. Winthrop Jr. House or Muttontown Meadows. It was purchased in 1950 by Lansdell Christie and renamed Christie House. In 1969, the house and its 183 acres were sold to Nassau County and became the headquarters of the Nassau Parks Conservancy.

The name "Muttontown" comes from the early use of the land for sheep grazing. In the 1600s, early English and Dutch settlers found the rolling hills ideal pastureland for thousands of sheep that provided mutton and wool.

The City of Long Beach

Long Beach is "The City by the Sea." It was founded in 1880 when the first Long Beach Hotel was built. The Long Island Rail Road arrived in 1882 and Long Beach, situated with the ocean on one side and the bay on the other, became a sea-side resort community. In 1922, it became a city, and remains one of only two cities on Long Island (Glen Cove is the other). The beach is 3.5 miles of pure white sand complemented by 2.2 miles of boardwalk from New York Avenue to Neptune Boulevard. Long Beach is only a half mile wide at its widest point. Many past seasonal summer homes are now year-round residences. After Superstorm Sandy in 2012, the City revitalized and redeveloped.

TOP RIGHT: National Boulevard, 1912.

BOTTOM RIGHT: Arcade at the Boardwalk.
Photos courtesy of The Long Beach Historical and Preservation Society.

BELOW: Long Beach welcome sign.
Photo by Denise Rafkind.

The Long Beach Boardwalk

Along the beach by the Atlantic Ocean, there is a 2.2-mile-long boardwalk. It was built in 1914 with the help of some elephants, and completely rebuilt in 2013 after the devastation of Superstorm Sandy. The Boardwalk is popular year-round. In winter and in summer, there are strollers, joggers, and bicycle riders.

Lido Club Hotel

The Lido Club Hotel in Long Beach opened in 1929, attracting stars of the day and their guests. Its famous pink stucco facade marked the east end of the Boardwalk. The hotel officially closed in 1981, and was converted to condominiums. The Lido Club Hotel is now the Lido Beach Towers. The former pink stucco is now gray, though the building retains its Moorish style.

It is rumored that the lyrics: "We walked on the beach beside that old hotel, They're tearing it down now, But it's just as well," from Billy Joel's 1986 song "This Is The Time," refers to the Lido Club Hotel.

TOP: Long Beach boardwalk, the beach, and the Atlantic Ocean.

LEFT: Lido Hotel, 1942.

Photos courtesy of The Long Beach Historical and Preservation Society.

Long Beach on the Beach

OPPOSITE PAGE: Long Beach Patrol.

TOP: Hotel Nassau opened in 1909 at West Broadway and National Boulevard. The location served as a military hospital during WWI, returning after as a hotel. Today it is the Ocean Club apartments.

LEFT: The beach is a year-round event. Shown are children playing on the beach sand, in the colder weather.
Photos courtesy of The Long Beach Historical and Preservation Society.

TOP RIGHT: Long Beach in the 1940s.
Photo courtesy of the Towers Family.

Nunley's, Baldwin

In 1940, Nunley's opened in Baldwin and became an iconic carousel and amusement park. Originally it was a carousel pavilion and restaurant, and later expanded to add amusement rides and a miniature golf course. It was a very popular family destination on Long Island's South Shore.

When it closed in 1995, Nunley's Carousel was rescued by Nassau County. It was beautifully restored and since 2009, the Carousel found a home and now operates at the Cradle of Aviation Museum in Garden City.

Nunley's Carousel

The carousel was built in 1912 by the company Stein and Goldstein for Golden City Park, in Canarsie, Brooklyn. It operated as Murphy's Carousel for 26 years. In 1939, third-generation amusement park impresario William Nunley purchased it and moved it to Sunrise Highway in Baldwin, and renamed it Nunley's Carousel.

The Carousel's Brass Ring

Nunley's Carousel is made up of painted wooden panels, 41 horses, two sit down chariots, a stand still lion, the original Wurlitzer organ, and the brass ring machine, (a wooden arm filled with silver and brass rings). The arm reaches out toward the carousel so that riders can reach out and grab the brass rings. If a patron grabs a brass ring, they win a free ride on the carousel.

A special soundtrack plays at the Carousel, which includes a tribute written by Long Island's Billy Joel, "Waltz No. 1, Op. 2 (Nunley's Carousel)." The instrumental is from Billy Joel's September, 2001, classical album *Opus 1-10 Fantasies & Delusions – Music for Solo Piano*, and was also in his 2002 Broadway musical and the original cast recording of *Movin' Out*.

ABOVE: Nunley's Carousel.
Photo by Denise Rafkind.

RIGHT: Nunley's green ride ticket.
Photo courtesy of Baldwin Historical Society.

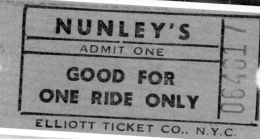

ABOVE: *Black Beauty, Nunley's Carousel,* watercolor painting by Michael White.

LEFT: *Nunley's Carousel and Amusements,* watercolor painting by Michael White.

Iconic paintings of Nunley's by artist Michael White

Artist Michael White says, "I came upon an online photo of my favorite Nunley's horse as it used to look in its old setting in Baldwin, and thought it the perfect source for a painting. When I posted the painting online, I was overwhelmed by the outpouring from Long Islanders who remembered the horse, carousel, and park with such fondness. It encouraged me to make more artworks of the brilliant carved horses from that miraculous little place."

Long Island Rail Road Mural

The memory of the Nunley's Carousel lives on today in Baldwin, in a 7-foot-long and 5-foot-wide acrylic mural at the Baldwin Long Island Rail Road station that was installed on April 22, 2019.

Artist Michael White describes, "I aimed for an image rich in detail and high dynamic impact, to be appreciated by zooming Sunrise Highway motorists and walking commuters alike."

All photos courtesy of Michael White.

ABOVE: Tiny pencils and this scorecard were key for any visit to Nunley's Mini Golf course.

LEFT: For many on Long Island, this ride was a person's first experience "driving a car."

BELOW: The arcade was filled with games for all ages. Families often played skee ball together.

All photos courtesy of Baldwin Historical Society.

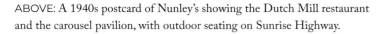

ABOVE: A 1940s postcard of Nunley's showing the Dutch Mill restaurant and the carousel pavilion, with outdoor seating on Sunrise Highway.

RIGHT: A day at Nunley's was not complete without a visit to the star attraction, an old fortune teller, much like the one featured in Tom Hank's movie *Big*.

Oceanside

The land that is now Oceanside was originally inhabited by the Rockaway Native Americans, followed by the Dutch, and then the English. Around 1682, the area became known as Christian Hook. In 1864, it was renamed Oceanville, followed by Ocean Side in 1890, and finally Oceanside in 1918.

Chwatsky's

Chwatsky's Department Store was located in the center of town on Long Beach Road in Oceanside. It was open from 1951 until it closed its doors in 2001. It was a popular destination for clothing and also the source for Boy and Girl Scout uniforms.

Oceanside Triangle "Trolley Stop 102" circa 1910.

Photo courtesy of 1960sailors.net.

Oceanside Liberty Lighthouse

Oceanside Liberty Lighthouse is a 25-foot-tall, decorative lighthouse at the Veterans Triangle of Long Beach Road, Lower Lincoln Avenue, and Davidson Avenue. The landmark location in the center of town was once a turnaround point for the trolley line, called "Trolley Stop 102."

Photo by Denise Rafkind.

The Oceanside General Merchandise Store, located on the corner of Davidson Avenue and Long Beach Road, was opened by brothers Morris and Herman "Hymie" Chwatsky in 1927. Most of the business was door-to-door. Pictured here is Hymie delivering in the business truck. Later, it was called the Oceanside General Variety Shoppe. In 1951, business expanded and transformed to the brick and mortar store known as Chwatsky's. *Photo courtesy of the Oceanside Library and Richard Woods.*

Roadside Rest, Oceanside

In 1921, the Roadside Rest on Long Beach Road in Oceanside was a fruit and vegetable stand. It was opened by brothers-in-law Leon Shor and Marty Hadfield. It was expanded in 1929 to a restaurant that sold frankfurters and seafood. Live entertainment by big bands offered dancing. Roadside Rest gained a national reputation when its musical entertainment was broadcast nightly by radio coast to coast. The Roadside Rest occupied a full city block and had a 3,000-person capacity. It was called "Long Island's Famous Family Rendezvous."

In the 1930s and the early 1940s, Shor and Hadfield owned and operated two "branch" locations. One was on Sunrise Highway in Merrick, called "the Island Rest." The other was in Miami Beach, Florida, where many native Long Islanders migrated to in the winter. In the mid-1940s, those two locations closed and Hadfield continued to operate the Oceanside location until the mid-1950s.

Photo courtesy of Howard B. Levy and 1960sailors.net.

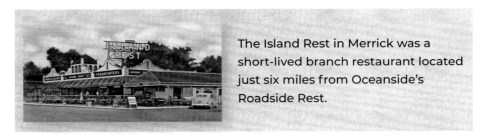

The Island Rest in Merrick was a short-lived branch restaurant located just six miles from Oceanside's Roadside Rest.

Nathan's Famous, Oceanside

In the 1950s, Roadside Rest was sold to Nathan Handwerker, the proprietor of Nathan's restaurant in Coney Island, Brooklyn. In 1957, it operated as Murray's Roadside Rest. On June 4, 1959, it opened officially as Nathan's Famous, Inc. and was the first Nathan's restaurant to open outside of Brooklyn. Many Brooklynites had started to migrate out to Long Island, and their favorite home-town hot dog followed. Families could also purchase tickets for Kiddieland Park, featuring entertaining rides for children.

Nathan's served a variety of foods that were unique in the area, including pizza, corn on the cob, lobster rolls, clams on the half shell, Ipswich fried clams, chow mein on a bun, and frog's legs. French fries and frankfurters with sauerkraut were most popular and hamburgers were also available. Each food category required customers to wait in a separate line. Families would designate one person to obtain the drinks, one for fries, one for hotdogs, and so on.

LEFT: *Nathan's Famous Oceanside* watercolor painting by Michael White. *Photo courtesy of Michael White.*

BOTTOM LEFT: Ticket for rides at Nathan's.

BOTTOM RIGHT: The paper cup from Nathan's instantly brings back a memory of soda, and French fries with a tiny, red fork.

Bottom photos courtesy of Howard B. Levy and 1960sailors.net.

In the 1960s, groups gathered weekly for either car nights or a biker's night where hundreds of motorcycles and their riders gathered in the parking lot. In 1971, Handwerker brought back entertainment, with banjos, sing-a-longs, jazz acts, and square dancing, along with kiddie entertainment.

By 1976, the 47-year-old building had deteriorated. It was demolished and a strip-mall shopping center was erected in its place. Nathan's re-opened at the north corner of Long Beach Road and Windsor Parkway. It was renowned for its arcade, home to all kinds of pinball. Into the 1980s, popular electronic video games were added such as Asteroids, Pac-Man and Space Invaders. Tuesday night was

"Motorcycle night" and Thursday night was "Classic Car night," where people filled the parking lot each week.

In June 2014, Nathan's closed the location and in 2015 opened a half mile down Long Beach Road in a smaller location on the corner of Merle Avenue, where it operates solely as a food restaurant.

The original Nathan's Famous

The original Nathan's Famous on Surf Avenue in Coney Island, Brooklyn, began in 1916 as a five-cent hot dog stand named for its founder, Nathan Handwerker (1892-1974). The original Nathan's still operates, and is the only Nathan's location that offers fried frog's legs, an original menu item since the 1950s.

The Nathan's Hot Dog Eating Contest has been held annually on July 4th since the 1970s. The current record as of 2021 is held by 14-time champion, Joey Chestnut, for eating 76 hot dogs (with buns) in 10 minutes.

The Mermaid Parade

Since 1983, the Mermaid Parade is the United State's Largest Art Parade. Held in the summer by Coney Island USA, the parade is a celebration of ancient mythology and honky-tonk rituals of the seaside. The parade showcases over 3,000 creative individuals and celebrates the community of Coney Island. Hundreds of thousands attend the amusement area for the parade.

The Mermaid Parade was founded with three goals: to bring mythology to life for local residents who live on streets named Mermaid and Neptune; to create self-esteem in a district that is often disregarded as "entertainment"; and to let artistic New Yorkers find self-expression in public. The parade has no ethnic, religious, or commercial aims, and features participants dressed in hand-made costumes based on themes and categories set in advance.

ABOVE: Nathan's June 8, 1947. *Photo courtesy of the Library of Congress.*

RIGHT: The 36th Annual Mermaid Parade in 2019, as floats and mermaid dancers pass by Nathan's Famous in Coney Island, Brooklyn. *Photo by Bill Barash.*

The Oyster Festival, Oyster Bay

ABOVE: Festival ship, *The John J. Harvey* and the Coast Guard at the Oyster Festival. *Photos by Bill Barash.*

In 1983, the Oyster Festival in Oyster Bay started out as a celebration of former U.S. President Theodore Roosevelt, whose family once owned a summer home in the community. Today it is the largest waterfront festival held on the East Coast of the United States. More than 150,000 people attend annually. Called simply the "Oysterfest" or the "O-Fest" by locals, the world-famous festival includes entertainment, parades, craft and artisan shows, and sailing tall ships. There is a food court where chefs and culinary professionals serve up unique oyster, clam and seafood items with traditional festival foods. The main attraction is of course oysters, and the festival always includes an iconic Oyster Eating and Oyster Shucking Contest. The festival is run by the Oyster Bay Charitable Fund and the Rotary Club of Oyster Bay. This annual tradition is held in mid-October. In 2020, it was held virtually due to the COVID-19 pandemic, and in 2021, it was cancelled for the first time in its history, due to the continuing pandemic.

New York World's Fair 1964-1965,
Flushing Meadows-Corona Park, Queens

Robert Moses served as president of the World's Fair Corporation and opened the fair on April 22, 1964. The 1964-1965 New York World's Fair ran for two six-month seasons, April 22 to October 18, 1964, and April 21 to October 17, 1965. Over 140 pavilions and 110 restaurants, representing 80 nations, 24 U.S. states and over 45 corporations had exhibits or attractions. The fair covered 646 acres of Flushing Meadows-Corona Park.

Dubbed a "universal and international" exposition, the fair's theme was "Peace Through Understanding." The theme was symbolized by a 12-story-high, stainless steel model of the earth called the Unisphere, built on the foundation of the Perisphere from the 1939 World's Fair. In 1964, adult admission price was $2.00 ($2.50 in 1965), and one dollar for children under 12 years of age.

Pavilions from U.S. states and American industry giants, including General Motors, IBM, Bell Systems, Westinghouse, Sinclair Oil, Ford, Parker Pen, DuPont, and Chunky Candy, educated and entertained over 51 million fair visitors.

TOP: The Unisphere from the World's Fair was constructed by U.S. Steel and still stands today.

Top photo by Bill Barash, left and inset photos by Max Henry Hubacher, courtesy of the New York Public Library.

The New York State Pavilion

The New York State Pavilion, constructed as the state's exhibit hall for the World's Fair, is also a prominent visible structure in the park. However, no new use for the building was found after the fair, and the building sat derelict and decaying for decades. In 1997, the ruins were featured in the movie, *Men in Black*. The New York State Pavilion was listed on the National Register of Historic Places in 2009.

ABOVE: The 1964-1965 World's Fair was the second World's Fair to be held at this location. The first was the 1939-1940 New York World's Fair that opened on April 30, 1939, coinciding with the 150th anniversary of the presidential inauguration of George Washington, which was in New York City, the original capitol of the United States.

Photos courtesy of the Farmingdale-Bethpage Historical Society and the Farmingdale Public Library Digital Photograph Collection.

Photo by Max Henry Hubacher, courtesy of the New York Public Library.

Old Bethpage Village Restoration

In 1963, Nassau County acquired the Powell property, a 165-acre farm along the Nassau-Suffolk border. The land was developed to preserve Long Island's architectural and rural history. The Powell Farmhouse, built in 1744 and inhabited until 1960, is the only building that was originally located at the site. Plainview's Manetto Hill Methodist Church was the first structure saved and moved to the property.

Old Bethpage Village Restoration opened on June 27, 1970. The living history museum is a 209-acre village of 51 historic buildings and seven reconstructions of homes, farms, and businesses. The site recreates life in a 19th-century American village with roots in the Dutch and English settlements of colonial Long Island. Costumed actors provide demonstrations of 19th-century life. The Noon Inn is a working tavern, and Layton's Store sells candy. The Bach Blacksmith Shop repairs ironworks used in the village. Farms depict typical agricultural practices from rural Long Island in the 1800s, including fields planted with crops, barns and outbuildings, gardens, and farm animals.

TOP: A colonial man stands by his velocipede, a human-powered land vehicle. This version of a bicycle is from the late 1800s.

ABOVE LEFT: The Kirby House, at Old Bethpage Village Restoration.

ABOVE: A demonstration of 19th-century life, a potter in colonial times used wheels to turn the clay as it was shaped.

All photos by Bill Barash.

The Long Island Fair

The pie baking contest winners at the annual Long Island Fair held at Old Bethpage Village Restoration. *Photo by Bill Barash.*

The Long Island Fair is a yearly tradition and was first held in 1842 by the Agricultural Society of Queens, Nassau, and Suffolk Counties, one of the oldest agricultural societies in the United States. Called the Queens County Fair, it was held every fall on vacant lots and members' farms. In 1866, the fair moved to its first permanent location at the County Court Complex at the intersection of Old Country Road and Washington Avenue in Mineola. The Fair's centerpiece was an Exhibition Hall. The large cruciform building with a high central tower capped by a grand eagle weathervane housed horticultural, agricultural, and domestic art displays.

In 1899, the year Nassau County was created, the name was changed to the Mineola Fair. As the population in Nassau County grew, the Fair was moved to the Roosevelt Raceway. It remained there until 1970 when it moved to its permanent location at the Old Bethpage Village Restoration and was renamed The Long Island Fair.

Since the Old Bethpage Village Restoration opened in 1970, the Long Island Fair has been held there every October. This agricultural, family-friendly fair shares the experience of old Long Island with tens of thousands of visitors who experience life on Long Island as it was in the 19th century.

Permanent fairgrounds completed in 1995 includes a replica of the Exhibition Hall from the Mineola Fair. The fair includes contests such as making scarecrows, pie bake-offs, vegetable, fruit, and flower competitions, and needlework and handcrafted hobby displays.

Powell Home

c. 1933. *Photo courtesy of Historic American Buildings Survey.*

In 1687, Thomas Powell was the first European settler in the Farmingdale area. On October 18, 1695, Powell purchased a 15-square-mile tract of land from three Native American tribes, the Marsapeque, Matinecoc, and Sacatogue. This was known as the Bethpage Purchase and includes what is now Farmingdale, Bethpage, Melville, North Massapequa, Old Bethpage, Plainedge, and Plainview. Powell died at Westbury, December 28, 1721. The Powell Home was built in the 1700s.

Bethpage

Powell called the land he purchased "Bethphage," because it was situated between two other places on Long Island, Jericho and Jerusalem, just as the biblical town of Bethphage (meaning "house of figs") was situated between Jericho and Jerusalem in Israel. The Long Island place formerly called Jerusalem is known today as Wantagh and Island Trees. Jericho retains the same name. Over time, the second letter H was dropped from the name, to spell Bethpage.

Main Street, Patchogue
and the 1976 Long Island Bicentennial Celebrations

Photo by Robert E. Miskosky, courtesy of Linda Bellafatto.

Celebrations for the Bicentennial occurred throughout all of Long Island. Shown here is a commemorative placard from The Phillips House in Rockville Centre.
Photo courtesy of the Rockville Centre Historical Society and the Phillips House Museum.

On July 9, 1976, the Patchogue Village "Big Bicentennial Blast Night" included the showing of antique automobiles and fire trucks. East Patchogue residents Robert E. Miskosky and Wilhelmina "Billie" Werderman Miskosky brought their 1947 Lincoln Zephyr convertible to the event.

Rose Jewelers was located at 74 East Main Street. The family-owned business known in the Hamptons for fine jewelry opened in 1945. The Patchogue store closed in 2014, and the Southampton store closed in 2018.

Falkoff Shoes at 66 East Main Street was a traditional shoe store, carrying the Stride-Rite brand. In 1980, Falkoff Shoes was purchased by Ralph Zegel, who was known as "Mr. Patchogue." Patchogue-born and Long Island-raised, Zegel was a 65-year member of the North Patchogue Fire Department. Falkoff's was run by the Zegel family until it closed in 2020. David's Shoe Emporium now stands in the location.

The "Spirit of '76" sign in the store window at the far right signals the 200th anniversary of the signing of the Declaration of Independence on July 4, 1776. In 1976, bicentennial celebrations were held in towns like Patchogue throughout Long Island and across the United States. The revelry didn't end on July 4th. Citizens celebrated all year long to mark this special milestone.

Tanner Park, Copiague

Tanner Park in the Town of Babylon is located on the Great South Bay. Known for hosting free summer concerts, it is also renowned for its athletic fields: baseball, football, lacrosse, softball, and soccer, and basketball and tennis courts. There is a boat launching station, a marina, picnic area, senior center, skateboard park, playground, fishing, and beach swimming. Tanner Park is the largest of 29 parks and beaches in the Town of Babylon. In 1962, General Foreman of the Town of Babylon Highway Department, Richard Tanner, surveyed the 93-acre park. The park was later named to honor Tanner, a Copiague resident.

The beauty of Tanner Park exemplified in a single tree by the waterfront. Locals call it the Sideways Tree. *Photo by Dyan Henn.*

Copiague is a hamlet in the Town of Babylon. As the home of the Massapequa Native Americans, English settlers purchased land from the tribes in 1657 and called it Copyag. In 1693 it was called Cuppuauge. Some called it Powell's, after one of its earliest landowners.

Legend has it that Chief Wyandanch sold the land that became Copiague to settlers, in exchange for "12 coats, 20 pounds of gunpowder, 20 hatchets and 20 knives." The settlers called the area Huntington South, which was the community's name when President George Washington visited in 1790 during his tour of Long Island. Later, it was known as East Amityville, and renamed Great Neck in the 1840s. Finally in 1895, the name Copiague was derived from a Native American term meaning "sheltered harbor," referring to the land hugging the shore of the Great South Bay.

Feller's Pond, Lindenhurst

Feller's Pond and surrounding land were donated by Otto F. Eichhammer in 1934.

Feeding the ducks is a collective memory shared by many Long Islanders. Although feeding waterfowl in the wild is now discouraged, in past decades this was a common occurrence in parks and at duck ponds such as Feller's Pond. *Photo by Dyan Henn.*

Robert Moses Causeway and the Great South Bay Bridge

On the Great South Bay Bridge, where you see the Robert Moses Causeway span across the Great South Bay, you feel part of Long Island's South Shore. On a clear day, you can faintly see the New York City skyline 60 miles off in the distance. The Bridge is often referred to as the "Robert Moses Bridge."

The Robert Moses Causeway opened in 1954 with a two-lane southbound span that was rebuilt in the late 1990s. The three-lane northbound span opened in 1968. The Causeway is an 8.10 mile parkway in Suffolk County connecting West Islip to the barrier beach islands (Jones Beach Island, Captree Island and western Fire Island). Until 1963, it was previously known as the Captree State Parkway.

Aerial photo taken from 3,500 feet. *Photo by David and Andria Rosen.*

Photo by Dyan Henn.

About the Bridge

The two-mile-long span across Great South Bay to Captree Island features a 600-foot-long main span, with a 60-foot clearance for boats. On either side of the main steel-arch span, a series of piles support the roadway 25 feet above the Great South Bay. The piles are arranged both vertically and diagonally. The diagonal piles, which are called "batter piles," resist the forces along the roadway such as those caused by vehicles stopping or starting, as well as those caused by the expansion and contraction of the bridge deck due to temperature changes.

Robert Moses

Robert Moses designed and executed the parkway system on Long Island. He was the President of the Long Island State Park Commission in 1924, and was one of the most influential planners of Long Island in the early 20th century. He managed the expansion of the park system by building a network of roads, or "parkways," to give the public access to the new parks. This shaped Long Island's roadways.

Moses was born December 18, 1888, and died July 29, 1981, in West Islip. His career in public works transformed the New York landscape, including the building of 35 highways, 12 bridges, numerous parks, the Lincoln Center for the Performing Arts in New York City, Shea Stadium, and the 1964-65 New York World's Fair.

Photo courtesy of the New York Public Library.

Sag Harbor Main Street,
Hampton Bays

Main Street was established in 1745. In the 1820s and 1830s, at the height of Sag Harbor's whaling days, Main Street was a cosmopolitan town center. In the 1950s, it was a blue-collar gathering place for residents. Main Street runs from the Long Wharf to the north and Jermain Avenue to the south.

Main Street, watercolor painting by Elizabeth Delury, 2007. *Photo courtesy of Elizabeth Delury.*
This Long Island moment in time was captured by Elizabeth Delury after she and her mother, Nellie Madeline Delury, were strolling along the quaint shops of Main Street in Sag Harbor. Nellie had seven children and seven grandchildren. Spending a cherished and rare mother-daughter shopping day prompted Elizabeth to preserve the moment in a painting. Elizabeth recalls seeing a waitress standing in the restaurant window, looking out towards the shoppers on Main Street.

Sagamore Hill, Cove Neck, Oyster Bay

Sagamore Hill was the home of the 26th President of the United States, Theodore Roosevelt, from 1885 until his death in 1919. Located in Cove Neck, Long Island, the 83-acre estate is known as the "Summer White House" of President Roosevelt.

In 1880, Roosevelt purchased farmlands in Cove Neck, a peninsula just east of Oyster Bay Village. In 1884, he hired New York City architects Lamb and Rich to design a large, sturdy, modern home. He planned to name the home "Leeholm" for his wife, Alice Hathaway Lee Roosevelt, but she died shortly after the birth of their daughter. Roosevelt pushed ahead with construction of the house, wanting to provide a proper home for his daughter. He changed the name to "Sagamore Hill." Sagamore is the Algonquin word for chieftain, meaning the head of the tribe.

In 1887, Roosevelt married Edith Kermit Carow. Over the next 30 years they raised six children at Sagamore Hill. The 23-room mansion remained their residence for their entire lives, and was Roosevelt's "Summer White House" for seven summers from 1902 until 1908. It played host to numerous visits from domestic and foreign dignitaries, and peace talks that helped draw an end to the Russo-Japanese War in 1905.

On January 6, 1919, at age 60, Theodore Roosevelt died at Sagamore Hill. Edith died on September 30, 1948, at the home at age 87.

On July 25, 1962, Congress established Sagamore Hill as a National Historic Site and the property was listed on the National Register of Historic Places on October 15, 1966.

ABOVE FAR LEFT: This felt banner souvenir was popular with elementary school students who visited Sagamore Hill on class field trips.

ABOVE LEFT: President Roosevelt at "Sagamore Hill," June 7, 1902.
Image courtesy of the New York Public Library.

OPPOSITE PAGE and ABOVE RIGHT: Sagamore Hill.
Photos by Bill Barash.

BOTTOM: Theodore Roosevelt's study/den in his home in Oyster Bay.
Photo courtesy of the New York Public Library.

Theodore Roosevelt Rough Rider Statue at the TR Triangle,
Oyster Bay

On October 30, 2010, the Theodore Roosevelt Rough Rider statue was placed in its permanent home at the 26th U.S. President's hometown of Oyster Bay. The two-and-a-half-ton sculptured bronze statue honors President Roosevelt's days as a Rough Rider, depicting Roosevelt with his horse, Little Texas. The statue is a replica and was cast from the mold of the original 1922 Rough Rider statue in Portland, Oregon, by American artist Alexander Phimister Proctor (1860-1950).

Before he was President of the United States, Roosevelt was the Assistant Secretary of the Navy. In 1898, he resigned to organize the "Rough Riders," the first U.S. Volunteer Cavalry in the Spanish-American War. The U.S. was fighting against Spain over its colonial policies with Cuba. Colonel Roosevelt received a posthumous Medal of Honor for leading the dual charges up Kettle Hill and San Juan Hill.

The Rough Rider Statue was rededicated at the triangle on the entrance to the Village of Oyster Bay, now known as the Theodore Roosevelt Triangle ("the TR Triangle"). The statue was originally dedicated on October 29, 2005, when it was temporarily placed across the street from its current location. The TR Triangle was designed by architects Reilly & Associates of Sea Cliff. They carried out a plan from 1918 to plant five trees honoring five local World War I veterans, including a memorial for Roosevelt's son, Quentin. The U.S. flag raised at the TR Triangle was flown over the USS Theodore Roosevelt aircraft carrier.

THEODORE ROOSEVELT
ROUGH RIDER STATUE

CAST FROM THE ORIGINAL 1922 MOLD
CREATED BY SCULPTOR
ALEXANDER PHIMISTER PROCTOR
1860 – 1950

DEDICATED
OCTOBER 29, 2005
AS THE
CENTENNIAL PROJECT
OF THE
ROTARY CLUB OF OYSTER BAY

RE-DEDICATED ON THIS SITE
BY THE
T.R. STATUE FUND
OCTOBER 30, 2010

Sam Ash

In 1924, Sam Ash Music began in Brooklyn, when musician, bandleader and violin teacher Sam Ash, and his wife, Rose, opened a music store. Their children, Jerome (Jerry), Paul and Marcia, would become active in the family business. In 1944, they expanded and opened a store on Utica Avenue in Brooklyn. The store offered sheet music, instrument repairs, phonographs and band instruments. In the 1950s, as rock and roll and rhythm and blues grew in popularity, Sam Ash was among the first stores to add brand name guitars such as Fender and Gibson. Fifteen-year-old Paul Ash supervised the record department.

In 1961, under the guidance of the second generation, Paul and Jerry expanded to Long Island, opening stores in Hempstead, and later, in Huntington. The Hempstead location was conveniently located near two popular places: Cooky's Steak Pub Restaurant and the A&S Department Store.

In 2006, Sam Ash was inducted into the Long Island Music Hall of Fame. In 2014, the Ash family third generation, Jerry's sons David, Richard and Sammy, took over management. The fourth generation currently works in the business as well.

Sam Ash is iconic for students of music, hobbyists, professional musicians and DJs, and for its recording and professional sound equipment. Their extensive range of sheet music included over 40,000 different titles. Long Islanders would often spend countless hours thumbing through the vast collection. It was also the place to discover new and strange instruments. Musicians could be found "testing out" a new guitar or jamming together in the showroom.

Today, Sam Ash Music is headquartered in Hicksville. It is the largest family-owned chain of musical instrument stores in the country, with 45 locations in 16 different states.

LEFT: The Hempstead Sheet Music Department, in the late 1960s.

ABOVE: Brooklyn location on Utica Avenue.

TOP: Sam Ash.

RIGHT: Jerry Ash.

All photos courtesy of Sam Ash Music stores and Sammy Ash.

Shea Stadium, Citi Field and the New York Mets,
Flushing, Queens

Shea was a venue for historic concerts. In August 1965, The Beatles opened their North American tour to an audience of over 55,000 screaming fans. In July 2008, Shea hosted its final concert called *The Last Play at Shea*. It was filmed as a documentary about Shea Stadium, performed by Billy Joel, with a guest appearance by legendary Beatle Sir Paul McCartney singing "Let it Be."

Shea Stadium

William A. Shea Municipal Stadium opened on April 17, 1964, in Flushing Meadows-Corona Park, Queens. It was a multi-purpose stadium that served as the home of Major League Baseball's New York Mets from 1964 to 2008, and for the New York Jets Football team from 1964 to 1983. Shea was responsible for bringing National League Baseball back to New York after the Brooklyn Dodgers and the New York Giants relocated to California in 1957. On opening day, over 50,000 people were in attendance. The stadium opened five days before the nearby 1964-1965 New York World's Fair.

The New York Yankees played their home games at Shea Stadium during the 1974 and 1975 seasons while Yankee Stadium was being renovated. The Mets, Yankees, Jets, and Giants all called Shea home in 1975, the only time in professional sports history that two baseball teams and two football teams shared the same facility in the same year.

LEFT: Shea Stadium, 1965.
Photo courtesy of The U.S. National Archives.

The New York Mets, one of baseball's first expansion teams, was founded in 1962. Prior to finding a home at Shea, the Mets played home games at the Polo Grounds in Manhattan for the 1962 and 1963 seasons.

The End of Shea Stadium

The stadium was dismantled in 2009. Seats, signs and other salvageable items were removed and put up for sale. Seats were offered for $869 per pair, representing a combination of the '86 and '69 Mets two World Series Championship years. The land was used to create parking lots for Citi Field, the new stadium built adjacent to where Shea once stood.

Citi Field

On March 29, 2009, Citi Field opened in Flushing Meadows-Corona Park, Queens. It is the home of the New York Mets (National League East division of Major League Baseball). The $850 million ballpark is named for Citigroup, who purchased the naming rights. On March 21, 2019, Citi Field changed its permanent address to 41 Seaver Way, to honor Mets Hall of Fame pitcher Tom Seaver, whose uniform number was 41.

Jackie Robinson, 1954.

Citi Field's front entrance is a rotunda named for Brooklyn Dodgers legend Jackie Robinson. To honor his life and accomplishments, in the rotunda's 160-foot-diameter floor, and etched into the archways, are words and images that defined Robinson's nine values: Courage, Excellence, Persistence, Justice, Teamwork, Commitment, Citizenship, Determination, and Integrity.

Photo by Bob Sandberg, courtesy of United States Library of Congress' Prints and Photographs division.

ABOVE: Citi Field, April 1, 2013. *Photo by Ashley Andujar, courtesy of The U.S. National Archives.*

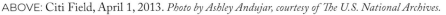

In Citi Field's parking lot is a plaque commemorating the location of Shea Stadium's home plate. There are additional plaques for the pitcher's mound, and bases.

Photo by Commandr Cody, courtesy of Creative Commons.

The first publication of *Newsday* was on September 3, 1940, in Hempstead. A daily publication, the newspaper serves Long Island and the surrounding metropolitan area. It is currently headquartered in Melville. The paper's slogan is "*Newsday*, Your Eye on LI." Previously, it was "*Newsday*, the Long Island Newspaper." *Newsday* has won 19 Pulitzer Prizes and has been a finalist an additional 21 times.

Through the years, *Newsday* has won many awards and has been recognized for its journalism from esteemed organizations such as the Silurians Press Club, the Deadline Club, the International News Media Association, the Associated Press Sports Editors Association, National Headliner Awards, and both the New York and Long Island Press Clubs. In addition, since 2012, *Newsday* has won 55 New York Emmy Awards.

Ownership

Newsday was founded by Alicia Patterson and her husband, Harry Guggenheim. After Patterson's death in 1963, Guggenheim became publisher and editor. In 1967, Guggenheim continued as president and editor-in-chief, but turned over the publisher position to Bill Moyers. As publisher of *Newsday* from 1967 to 1970, Moyers brought aboard writers including Pete Hamill, Daniel Patrick Moynihan, and Saul Bellow, and led the paper to two Pulitzer Prizes. In 1968, Guggenheim sold his majority share to the Times-Mirror Company. In June 2000, Times-Mirror merged with the Tribune

TOP: Alicia Patterson, co-founder and longtime editor and publisher of *Newsday*, starts the presses on the first issue of the Long Island newspaper at the Hempstead plant on September 3, 1940.

LEFT: *Newsday*'s plant on Stewart Avenue in Garden City on Sept. 29, 1979.
Photo by Naomi Lasdon.

All photos courtesy of Newsday.

Company, partnering *Newsday* with the New York City television station WPIX (Channel 11). On July 29, 2008, Cablevision purchased *Newsday*. In 2016, Altice, a telecoms company, bought Cablevision, including *Newsday* and the cable station News 12. Altice then sold a 75 per cent majority stake in *Newsday* back to Cablevision's former owner, Charles Dolan, and his son Patrick. Patrick Dolan became the CEO of *Newsday*. In July, 2018, Altice disposed of its remaining stake in *Newsday*. Charles Dolan transferred his shares to his son, and Patrick Dolan became the sole owner of *Newsday*.

Newsday Carriers

Home delivery of *Newsday* was done seven days a week by paper carriers who were often kids. For many, delivering newspapers was their first paying job. Carriers worked every day after school, on weekends, and in all weather conditions. Papers were delivered by hand, and the carriers walked or rode a bicycle to bring each paper to the door or driveway of a subscriber's home. Each carrier had a route. Payment for the paper was collected weekly or monthly, of which carriers received a per-customer fee, and hopefully a tip. Carriers marketed subscriptions, added customers to their routes, and therefore added to their income. Eventually this was phased out and adults in vehicles handled early morning deliveries.

Modern Trends

Moving into its new headquarters in the summer of 2020, *Newsday* made a significant investment in video. Its new multimedia facility includes a state-of-the-art broadcast production studio and a space capable of live-streaming video productions with an audience. The cutting-edge facilities strengthen the organization's commitment to new types of content and creative storytelling through video productions, interviews, documentaries, and multipart series, to reach new audiences through a 21st-century lens.

TOP RIGHT: *Newsday* carrier Parry Vienna, 15, of Huntington Station, breaks through a snow bank to demonstrate her delivery technique on February 12, 1983. *Photo by Ari Mintz.*

BOTTOM RIGHT: A *Newsday* carrier uses a sled to help him deliver papers in the snow.

All photos courtesy of Newsday.

Suffolk County Almshouse Hay Barn,
Suffolk County Farm, Yaphank

Top photo by Mike J. Maietta.

Suffolk County Farm was established in 1870, when Suffolk County purchased 170 acres of cultivated land and woodland to build an almshouse for the needy. The Almshouse Hay Barn, a multi-story structure with a broad gable roof and wood shingle sheathing, was built in 1871, in the center of the Suffolk County Farm in Yaphank to store hay and straw and house livestock.

Almshouse residents provided agricultural labor to make the farm self-sufficient. In the 1940s, labor was supplied by county prison inmates and the farm supplied food, meat and vegetables for county facilities. In the 1960s, the Suffolk County Farm became an educational resource for county residents where agriculture, nutrition, history and environmental issues were taught. The Almshouse Hay Barn was added to the National Register of Historic Places in 1986.

The Stony Brook Grist Mill, Stony Brook

Built in 1751, The Stony Brook Grist Mill is Long Island's most completely equipped working mill, and stands today as an example of innovation.

The structure is post and beam Dutch-style frame construction. The mill operates to grind grains (oats, corn, wheat and barley) to flour. This was integral for commerce, as flour was much easier to transport than wheat or corn.

During the Revolutionary War, the grains ground at the Mill fed soldiers. In the 19th century, wine grapes were pressed at the Mill. In the 1940s "natural stoned flour" was produced and shipped throughout all 48 American states. The Grist Mill is a designated site on the New York State Revolutionary War Trail, and is listed on the National and New York State Registers of Historic Places.

Grist Mill, date unknown, but prior to 1952.
Photo courtesy of Albertype Company, Brooklyn, NY.

Photo by Kathleen Balsamo.

Sunrise Village / Sunrise Bavarian Village, Bellmore

Built in the 1920s, the Sunrise Bavarian Village (later called Sunrise Village) was a restaurant, dance hall, and beer garden on Sunrise Highway in Bellmore. It was owned by Frank Foerch and Paul Larm. There was a dance floor and stage with several nightly shows. In 1938, it boasted a sensational "Bavarian-American Floor Show – The Largest Floor Show on Long Island." A full-course deluxe dinner cost only one dollar.

In 1953, it was purchased by Bellmore resident Herman Wedel, who owned a nightclub on Merrick Road called The South Shore Terrace. In 1959, he closed the Terrace to focus on Sunrise Village. Shows became more continental, featuring acts including Frank Sinatra Jr. and Bobby Rydell. Madeline Kahn started her singing career at Sunrise Village.

Sunrise Village accommodated large events. Herman and his wife, Gisel, would serve up to 600 people at one time. In the late 1970s, an orchestra played while dancers did the "Can-Can." Their traditional Oktoberfests were legendary. After the death of her husband in 1976, Mrs. Wedel continued to operate the restaurant until it closed on December 31, 1978. The building was torn down and eventually replaced by a supermarket.

Photos courtesy of Oak Chalet and the Wedel family.

Oak Chalet, Bellmore

Since 1981, The Oak Chalet Restaurant on Bellmore Avenue has been owned and operated by the former owner of the Sunrise Village, Gigi (Gisel) Wedel, and Dieter Reinking. Gigi's children, Hewy and Susan Wedel, manage the restaurant which features chalet-styled decor with a fireplace, wooden tables and chairs. The furniture was handmade by the family and hearts are carved into every chair. The menu includes German-Continental fare, as well as American favorites, beer, and liquors. To celebrate Oktoberfest, the staff dresses in authentic German costumes; there are accordion players, German music, and German food.

Sweet Hollow Creamery and Milk Home Delivery on Long Island, Farmingdale

The Sweet Hollow Creamery was located on Alexander Avenue in Farmingdale, near Route 110. Early each morning, milkmen would deliver glass bottles filled with fresh milk. The milkmen would also remove empty bottles from metal boxes outside homes.

Prior to the development of commercial farms, people used to get their milk from their own cows. The first milk home deliveries date back to 1785, in Vermont. Milkmen would travel from dairy farms and fill containers at individual residences. Before refrigeration, perishable items were delivered daily to prevent spoilage before the dairy could be consumed.

The first glass milk bottle, called the Lester Milk Jar, was patented in 1878. Milk was sold in bottles starting in 1879. In 1884, Henry D. Thatcher developed a bottle with a cap, and by the 1920s, designs and advertisements were etched into the glass.

In the 1950s, glass became heavy and hard to manage for transport deliveries. It was also difficult to clean the bottles properly for reuse. In the 1960s, plastic milk jugs replaced the smaller glass bottles, and disposable milk cartons were used. The milkmen became obsolete as more homes had refrigerators, and jugs allowed the purchase of a larger quantity of milk at one time. The increase of grocery stores also made it easier for people to pick up dairy products when they purchased their groceries.

TOP: The Sweet Hollow Creamery milk delivery truck that would bring fresh milk to homes daily.

Photo by Rietheimer, courtesy of Farmingdale-Bethpage Historical Society and the Farmingdale Public Library Digital Photograph Collection.

TOP INSET: A milk bottle cap.

RIGHT INSET: A glass bottle.

LEFT INSET: The metal milk box found outside Long Island homes.

Long Island Game Farm Wildlife Park and Children's Zoo, Manorville

In 1970, the Long Island Game Farm was founded by Stanley and Diane Novak, who built the farm after being inspired by the Catskill Game Farm in upstate New York. Admission was $2 for adults and $1.50 for children.

The Game Farm has always been family run by the Novak family and their daughters Susan and Melinda. Stanley died in 1999, and Susan managed the park until her death in 2001. Diane retired in 2019. Melinda, who grew up from age nine in the farmhouse, currently runs the farm. The original farmhouse serves today as the administrative office.

The 29-acre farm dates back to 1900, and is home to over 200 animals, including buffalo, ostrich, emu, deer, wallabies, zebras, lemurs, and giraffes. Some of the animals are "snow birds" and spend the winter in Florida. It is the largest combined children's zoo and wildlife park on Long Island. The petting zoo allows visitors to pet, cuddle and bottle feed the baby animals such as goats, deer, sheep, and giraffes, creating indelible memories for children and adults.

For many Long Islanders, visiting the Long Island Game Farm is a yearly tradition. It is a destination for school class and summer camp trips to learn about wildlife and domesticated animals in their natural environment. Many second and third generations return to share their experiences with their children and grandchildren.

ABOVE: The Long Island Game Farmhouse was the Novak family home when the Game Farm opened.

Photos courtesy of Michael White.

Photo courtesy of Lisa J. Levy.

Wetson's

Wetson's Hamburgers, watercolor painting by Michael White. *Photo courtesy of Michael White.*

In 1959, brothers Herbert (Herb) and Errol Wetanson opened their first hamburger restaurant named Wetson's on Hempstead Turnpike in Levittown, in what was a closed Mayflower coffee and donut shop. Wetson's would expand to 70 locations in the New York area, mostly on Long Island, before merging with Nathan's Famous restaurants in 1975. Wetson's was known for the "Big W" burger, clown mascots Wetty and Sonny, and slogans "Look for the Orange Circles" and "Buy a Bagful." Many Long Islanders grew up looking for the rooftop orange neon rings of their favorite burger place. It was a popular spot where families would stop to eat after Little League games.

Walt Whitman

Widely recognized as America's greatest poet, Walt Whitman's writings are treasured for capturing the nation's spirit during the nineteenth century and examining some of the era's most significant events, including westward expansion, immigration, slavery, and the Civil War.

Walter Whitman was born on May 31, 1819, in a small farmhouse in West Hills, in the town of Huntington. His ancestors and family had lived in the South Huntington area for over 125 years. The second of nine children, he was called "Walt" to distinguish him from his father. Walter Whitman Sr., a skilled carpenter, built the farmhouse upon his marriage to Louisa Van Velsor in 1816.

Walt Jr. took his first job at age twelve as a printer's devil (an apprentice) at *The Long Island Patriot*. His career spanned journalism and writing conventional poetry, short

ABOVE: Walt Whitman Birthplace, 1924.
Photo courtesy of the Walt Whitman Birthplace Association (WWBA).

TOP: Walt Whitman's Birthplace is a State Historic Site listed on the National Register of Historic Places.
Photo by Denise Rafkind, used with permission of the Walt Whitman Birthplace Association (WWBA).

stories, and a novel. He also worked as a teacher in eight different school districts throughout the western half of Long Island. In 1838, he founded Huntington's weekly newspaper, *The Long-Islander*.

After 1841, Whitman returned to journalism full-time until 1859. He held editorial positions on seven different newspapers, four of them on Long Island, and two in New York City, including *The Long Island Star*, 1845; *The Brooklyn Weekly Eagle*, 1846-1848; *The Brooklyn Freeman*, 1848-1849; and the *Brooklyn Daily Times*, 1857-1859. In all of these positions he was an outspoken advocate of social, economic, and political reform in both local and national issues.

He has been hailed as the first "poet of democracy" in the United States, reflecting his ability to write in a singularly American character. In 1855, Whitman published the first edition of *Leaves of Grass*, a thin volume of poems written in a highly innovative style, inspired in part by his travels through the American frontier.

Several locations on Long Island honor his name, including Walt Whitman High School in Huntington Station, the Walt Whitman Shops (formerly called "Walt Whitman Mall") in Huntington Station, and Walt Whitman Road, located in Huntington Station and Melville.

LEFT: The eight-foot bronze statue of Walt Whitman with Butterfly was sculpted by artist John Giannotti.

RIGHT: *Leaves of Grass* quotation.

Photos by Denise Rafkind, used with permission of the Walt Whitman Birthplace Association (WWBA).

Whisper the Smithtown Bull

Since 1941, at the intersection of Routes 25 and 25A, stands Smithtown's famous landmark: the monument of Whisper the Bull.

It is a legend that in 1663 Richard Smith, an early settler of Southampton, made a deal with the local Native Americans and rode around Long Island on his trusty bull, Whisper, to claim the 55 square miles of land that would become Smithtown. Another version is that Richard Smith assisted in the recovery of a Montauk's Chief's daughter, and in reward, the Montauk Sachem granted him all the land he could encircle in a day by riding a bull. Probably more factual is that Smith obtained a deed from a friend, Lion Gardiner, who had obtained it from the Montauk Sachem. The name Whisper may also be from the legend, or, may be the result of a contest naming the monument from local elementary school students.

The statue was designed by architect Lawrence Smith Butler, a descendant of Richard Smith. The bronze Whisper statute measures 14 feet long, 9 feet tall and weighs over five tons. Whisper's coloring has aged to a greenish hue and remains the landmark of Smithtown.

LEGENDS & LORE
SMITH'S BULL RIDE
TOWN LIMITS DETERMINED BY DISTANCE OF ONE DAY RIDE. LAND WAS GIFT OF MONTAUK CHIEF FOR ASSISTANCE IN RETURN OF KIDNAPPED DAUGHTER.
NEW YORK FOLKLORE
WILLIAM C. POMEROY FOUNDATION 2019   61

TOP: Whisper, the Bull.
Photo by Kathleen Balsamo.

LEFT: "Legends & Lore" roadside markers and plaques celebrate community history throughout the United States.

Bayard Cutting Arboretum, Great River

ABOVE: The Bayard Cutting Arboretum remains an oasis of beauty where trees and plantings are cultivated and preserved, honoring the efforts of Bayard Cutting who first planted the conifers. Pictured here are small ornamental trees, flowering ornamental shrubs like hydrangeas and dwarf conifers, and perennials such as catmint, and an assortment of ornamental grasses. Within the collection are several trees that are the largest of their species in this area. The arboretum includes cultivated gardens, trees, plants, and shrubs that have been imported from all over the world, and serves as a sanctuary for small wildlife and aquatic birds.
Photo by Bill Barash.

Frederick Law Olmsted collaborated with Englishman Calvert Vaux to design and plan urban park systems. In 1863, they were the first to adopt a professional title of "landscape architect." Other renowned parks they designed include Central Park in New York City in 1858, and Prospect Park in Brooklyn, from 1865-1873.

The Bayard Cutting Arboretum consists of 691 acres situated on the Connetquot River. It was designed in 1886 by landscape architect Frederick Law Olmsted.

The land had been part of the Great River Estate known as Westbrook. William Bayard Cutting and his brother, Fulton, had started the sugar beet industry in the United States in 1888. Cutting was also a builder of railroads, operated the ferries of New York City, and developed a part of the south Brooklyn waterfront.

On June 18, 1936, The Bayard Cutting Arboretum was donated to the Long Island State Park Region by the Cutting family in memory of William Bayard Cutting, "to provide an oasis of beauty and quiet for the pleasure, rest and refreshment of those who delight in outdoor beauty; and to bring about a greater appreciation and understanding of the value and importance of informal planting."

The arboretum is not a traditional park, but rather a "museum of trees" that continues to preserve the amenities of the native landscape of Long Island. Bayard Cutting Arboretum State Park is one of the last remaining estates on the South Shore of Long Island. It was added to the National Register of Historic Places in 1973.

RIGHT: The Bayard Cutting Manor House, 1956. It was designed by architect Charles C. Haight as the Cutting family's residence. The 30-room mansion is typical of estate life in the 1920s and 1930s, boasting magnificent fireplaces, detailed woodworking, stained glass windows, and an open porch overlooking the Connetquot River.
Photo by Max Henry Hubacher, courtesy of the New York Public Library.

Houses of Worship

Agudas Achim, Setauket

In 1896, Agudas Achim was the first building constructed for use as a synagogue in Suffolk County. The building is known as "Shalom Hall." It is currently owned by Setauket United Methodist Church and used as a thrift store.

Photo courtesy of Brad Kolodny.

BAPS Shri Swaminarayan Mandir, Melville

On October 9, 2016, the BAPS Shri Swaminarayan Mandir was inaugurated in Melville. The 48,000-square-foot Mandir was the first building on Long Island to be constructed specifically as a Hindu house of worship. BAPS stands for Bochasanwasi Shri Akshar Purushottam Swaminarayan Sanstha, a Hindu denomination which had built the world's largest Hindu Mandir, in New Delhi, India. The Long Island Mandir is one of 112 BAPS Hindu Mandirs across North America.

ABOVE: BAPS Swaminarayan Mandir in Melville adds to the architectural, social, humanitarian and spiritual landscape of Long Island.

RIGHT: Mandir Moods, "Shikhars" refers to the top architectural points or peaks on Mandir buildings.

Photos courtesy of the BAPS Swaminarayan Mandir.

Basilica Parish of the Sacred Hearts of Jesus and Mary, Southampton

The parish, originally a mission church of St. Andrew's in Sag Harbor, was established in 1896. The current church structure in Southampton was erected in 1907. It was designated by the Vatican as a Minor Basilica in 2012, making it the first Roman Catholic Basilica on Long Island. This recognition was based upon the church's historical and architectural significance as well as its role in the formation of Catholicism in the community. Situated in the heart of the Hamptons, Sacred Hearts of Jesus and Mary joined 72 other churches across the country when it received this distinguished honor.
Photo by Leonard J. DeFrancisci.

B'nai Sholom, Rockville Centre

In 1915, B'nai Sholom in Rockville Centre was the first building constructed for use as a synagogue in Nassau County. It was located on Windsor Avenue near Merrick Road. The Windsor building was torn down after the congregation opened at its current location on Hempstead Avenue, in 1949. The congregation is currently known as B'nai Sholom Beth-David following a merger with Congregation Beth David in Lynbrook on March 4, 2011.
Photo courtesy of Brad Kolodny.

The Church of Jesus Christ of Latter-day Saints, Plainview

The Church of Jesus Christ of Latter-day Saints (LDS) is located on Washington Avenue. The building, known as the Plainview New York Stake Center, began as the Mormon Pavilion at the New York State World's Fair of 1964-1965. Over 500 missionaries worked in the pavilion which received an estimated 5.5 million visitors. The pavilion was specially constructed so that parts could be used later as a meeting house once the World's Fair ended. The 36 concrete panels that comprised the pavilion walls, each weighing 12 tons, were moved to Plainview. In 1970, the meeting house was rededicated by LDS President Harold B. Lee. *Photo by Doug Leibowitz.*

First Presbyterian Church at Christian Hook, Oceanside

The First Presbyterian Church at Christian Hook was the first church in Oceanside, constructed in 1871. Christian Hook was the former name of Oceanside. Reverend Marcus Burr served as the church's first minister. For several years prior to the church's construction, Burr preached in the morning at a Freeport church and then walked four miles to hold Sunday afternoon services in Oceanside across the street from where the church would eventually stand. As part of the 150th anniversary celebration in 2021, parishioners met in Freeport and drove four miles to First Presbyterian in Oceanside to honor Burr's weekly walk.

Photo courtesy of First Presbyterian Church at Christian Hook.

Greek Orthodox Cathedral of St. Paul, Hempstead

On June 13, 1945, The Orthodox Greek Catholic Community of Nassau and Suffolk Counties, New York, Inc. was founded. In 1950, the first Saint Paul's Church was erected on Greenwich Street in Hempstead. In 1955, a larger Church and Complex was built on Cathedral Avenue. Archbishop Iakovos of America officiated at the laying of the cornerstone in 1959. The Church is home to the "Lamenting Mother of God." The venerated icon received worldwide attention on March 16, 1960, when it was seen to tear. The Ecumenical Patriarchate proclaimed it to be a "Sign of Divine Providence," and the icon was moved from Island Park to be permanently enshrined in the cathedral. *Photo by Bill Kallinikos.*

Selden Masjid The Islamic Association of Long Island, Selden

Founded in 1974, the Selden Masjid is the oldest chartered mosque on Long Island. Renovations were completed in 2012 to include a new, modern building for the Islamic house of worship. *Image not available.*

Shiloh Baptist Church, Rockville Centre

Shiloh was the first Black Baptist Church in Nassau County to own property. In June 1907, Sister Glendora Hankins organized the first Black Baptist Church in Rockville Centre. On July 25, 1907, Shiloh Baptist Church was incorporated. In 1909, the church purchased a lot at 87 Banks Avenue, and a small-framed structure was moved to the location. In 1945, Shiloh purchased property on the corner of North Centre Avenue and Willoughby Street, the site of the present-day church. The new Shiloh Church was completed in June 1954, and dedicated on June 22, 1958.

On March 26, 1968, Reverend Dr. Martin Luther King, Jr., visited the Shiloh Church. He delivered a speech about his vision for the civil rights movement and the Poor People's Campaign he had recently founded, and the planned March on Washington for April. Tragically, he never made it to the march as he was assassinated just nine days later, on April 4, 1968.

Reverend Morgan M. Days led the church from 1937 to until 1985. He died in 1987; the Village of Rockville Centre honored him by changing the name of Willoughby Street to Morgan Days Lane.

Congregants in front of Temple Mischan Israel, 1900. *Photo courtesy of Temple Adas Israel.*

Temple Adas Israel, Sag Harbor

Temple Adas Israel is a Reform Jewish synagogue in Sag Harbor. It is the oldest continuously used synagogue building on Long Island. The synagogue was first utilized for services as Temple Mishcan Israel on September 23, 1900. There was a merger in 1918 with the Independent Jewish Association and the congregation was renamed Adas Israel.

LEFT: The original Shiloh Baptist Church location at 87 Banks Avenue, Rockville Centre. 1939.

ABOVE: Reverend Dr. Martin Luther King, Jr. *Photo by Marion S. Trikosko, courtesy of the Library of Congress.*

Photo courtesy of Brad Kolodny.

Services at Temple Avodah, Oceanside, 2016. *Photo by Stacy Mandel Kaplan.*

Temple Avodah, Oceanside

In 1955, at Temple Avodah in Oceanside, 31-year-old Betty Robbins was the first woman to be officially designated as a cantor in a Jewish Synagogue, shattering 5,000 years of Jewish tradition. Previously, only Julie Rosewald (1847-1906), had unofficially served as cantor at Temple Emanu-El in San Francisco from 1884 to 1893.

Robbins (1924-2004) was born in Greece, grew up in Poland, and sang in boys' choirs. As a child, girls were not taught in synagogues, so she studied behind a curtain during the boys' lessons. After fleeing Poland, she emigrated to Australia, where she married a U.S. Army Air Corps corporal. In 1951, Robbins and her husband moved from Australia to Oceanside. Along with their four children, they became members at Temple Avodah, a Reform Congregation on Long Island's South Shore. Robbins was the cantor at the High Holiday Services on September 15, 1955.

Trinity Evangelical Lutheran Church, Rocky Point

On Route 25-A in Rocky Point stands the Trinity Evangelical Lutheran Church, a congregation of the Metropolitan New York Synod of the Evangelical Lutheran Church in America. It was built in the 1950s. The church is known fondly as "The Fish Church" because the building's unique shape appears to many as a large fish. In reality, the church is in the shape of an equilateral triangle, a Christian symbol of the Trinity manifesting the universal Christian doctrine of the triune God.

Beacon Theatre, Port Washington

The Beacon Theatre, located on Port Washington's Main Street, opened on October 15, 1927. It was a single screen movie house with a stage and over 1,600 seats. During WWII, the theatre was used as a donation point for civilian scrap metal drives. The Beacon Theatre attracted famous movie stars such as Bette Davis and Olivia de Havilland. It proudly boasted the motto "Where the better pictures are shown." The location became a seven-plex theater in the 1980s, and closed in 2018.

RIGHT: A large crowd outside the theatre at 116 Main Street. The marquee reads: *The Great Garrick*, starring Brian Aherne and Olivia de Havilland; *Breakfast for Two* starring Barbara Stanwyck and Herbert Marshall, 1937. *Photo by Stanley Gerard Mason, Stanley Mason Studio, courtesy of The History Center, The Port Washington Public Library.*

Riviera Bath Club, Port Washington

Built in 1925, the Riviera Bath Club was located at 43 Orchard Beach Boulevard in Port Washington/Manorhaven. The club was first known as the North Hempstead Yacht Club before the name was changed to the Columbia Yacht Club. Under new ownership, it became the Riviera Bath Club. It included a swimming pool, cabanas, a restaurant and a marina. Famous crooners of the day, including Perry Como, made appearances there, arriving by boat from New York City. A popular locale of its day, it was considered "Long Island Sound's most modern and complete yachting facility." The Riviera Restaurant and Bath Club was destroyed by fire on January 9, 1974.

LEFT: The swimming pool at the Riviera Bath Club. 1960. On July 17th, 1960, photographer Stanley Mason ventured out from his studio on Main Street and photographed this woman at a swim meet at the Riviera Bath Club, capturing her graceful dive into the pool. *Photo by Stanley Gerard Mason, Stanley Mason Studio, courtesy of The History Center, The Port Washington Public Library.*

Brooklyn Bridge

The Brooklyn Bridge was completed on May 24, 1883. It was the first fixed crossing constructed across the East River to connect Long Island with Manhattan Island. Before the Brooklyn Bridge, the only means of travel between Long Island and the rest of the United States was by boat or ship. It was originally called the New York and Brooklyn Bridge or the East River Bridge, but in 1915 it was officially renamed the Brooklyn Bridge. Construction started in 1870 and took 13 years to complete.

The Bridge is a hybrid cable-stayed/suspension bridge. In 1883, it was the longest suspension bridge in the world, with a main span of 1,595.5 feet and a deck of 127 feet above the water. It was designed by architect John A. Roebling, with contributions by his son, Project Chief Engineer Washington Roebling, and Washington's wife, Engineer Emily Warren Roebling. The stone towers are neo-Gothic, with characteristic pointed arches.

The Brooklyn Bridge carried horse-drawn vehicles and had elevated railway lines until 1950. An elevated pedestrian and cycling promenade runs 18 feet above and between the vehicle roadways. In 1971, a centerline was painted to separate cyclists from pedestrians. This was one of New York City's first dedicated bicycle lanes. Only passenger vehicles, bicycles, and pedestrians are allowed to travel on the bridge. It underwent renovations in the 1950s, 1980s, and 2010s. It is one of four toll-free bridges that now connect Manhattan and Long Island. The other three are the Manhattan, Williamsburg, and Queensboro Bridges. It is a National Historic Landmark, a New York City landmark, and a National Historic Civil Engineering Landmark.

ABOVE: The Brooklyn Bridge Promenade, circa 1910-1919.
Photo courtesy of the Library of Congress.

OPPOSITE PAGE: The Brooklyn Bridge spanning the East River. Shown in the distance on the Manhattan side of the Brooklyn Bridge is One World Trade Center. 2019.
Photo by Bill Barash.

One World Trade Center

Across the East River on the Manhattan side of the Brooklyn Bridge is One World Trade Center, also known as One WTC, and formerly called the Freedom Tower. At 1,776 feet it is the tallest building in the United States, and the seventh tallest building in the world. It stands south of the original Twin Towers where the World Trade Center stood before it was destroyed by terrorist attacks on September 11th, 2001. The height is a deliberate reference to 1776, the year that the U.S. Declaration of Independence was signed. One WTC opened on November 3, 2014, and was designed by Architect David Childs of Skidmore, Owings & Merrill.

Argyle Theatre, Babylon

In 1921, a newspaper article in the *Babylon Leader* announced plans for a "$100,000 Theatre for Main Street." With a 1,500-seat capacity, the new Capitol Theatre was expected to be "the finest theatre on the South Side." The new entertainment venue would benefit residents, and help Babylon become a more attractive summer resort for vacationers. A playbill in 1923 advertised daily performances ranging from vaudeville to adaptations of Broadway shows such as *The Hero* and *East Side West Side*.

In 1925, the theatre reopened under new ownership as the Babylon Theatre, and delighted audiences with its many modern improvements which included a flashy electrical marquee. An advertising campaign in the surrounding communities was so successful that 500 people had to be turned away on opening night. It was obvious that the Babylon Theatre was poised for great success.

Throughout the following decades, the Babylon Theatre survived two fires and several different owners. It continued to operate as a modern cinema house until 2014.

In the spring of 2018, a newly renovated Argyle Theatre opened with the musical *Guys and Dolls*, the first show in a full roster of musicals, concerts, comedies, and other performances. Each year, the Argyle presents six main stage productions featuring performers from the Actors Equity Association, the union for professional stage actors.

The much-anticipated performance venue has been brought back to life by Seaford residents Mark and Dylan Perlman, the father-and-son duo behind the $5 million project. The Perlmans had long dreamed of bringing high-quality live theatre to Long Island's South Shore and found the ideal setting on Main Street in the beautiful Village of Babylon.

Renovations to the interior and exterior of the Argyle were extensive. In the summer of 2021, the theatre reopened after a long closure due to the COVID-19 pandemic, and continues to operate to this day.

"The support and good wishes of residents and businesses on Long Island and the tri-state area have been overwhelming," said Mark Perlman. "We all share the joy of this victory as Babylon's Main Street lights up once again with exhilarating live performances at the Argyle Theatre."

TOP: January 2022, World Premiere of *PUNK ROCK GIRL* with book and arrangements by Tony-nominated Long Island Composer Joe Iconis. *Photo by Richard Termine.*

ABOVE: The Theatre as it was in 1923 upon original opening. *Photo courtesy of the Argyle Theatre.*

RIGHT: The Theatre just before reopening as the Argyle in 2018. *Photo courtesy of the Argyle Theatre.*

Ray Romano house

For nine seasons, 320 Fowler Road, Lynbrook was home to Ray Barone's television family, who lived just across the street from Barone's parents. From 1996 to 2005, viewers watched *Everybody Loves Raymond*, the "comical everyday life of sports columnist Ray Barone and his dysfunctional family." In reality, the house was located at 135 Margaret Boulevard in Merrick, owned by the Mulligan family. Rob Mulligan tells the story of how his Long Island childhood home became a piece of television history:

ABOVE: The home at 135 Margaret Boulevard, Merrick, known on television as 360 Fowler Road, Lynbrook. 1996.

INSET: The original home in 1976. *Photo courtesy of Rob Mulligan.*

By Rob Mulligan

In 1965, my family relocated from Brooklyn to Merrick. In 1976, my mom, Helene, and step-father, Sandy, downsized to a charming Cape Cod-style house at 135 Margaret Boulevard. From sixth grade through my college years, this was the house I called home.

In 1996, a young man who lived across the street told my mom that he was working on the production of a new television show. He thought our house was perfect to create the image of a nice, middle-class suburban home. He offered $500 to film the exterior of our house. Mom said, "Sure, why not." The crew filmed and mom got her check, which she promptly donated to her church.

When the show was picked up for a full season, our neighbor hoped to film our house from different angles and in different settings. For this, mom would be paid $3,500! Once again, mom donated the entire amount to her church.

Throughout this process, my mom never mentioned this to me or my four older brothers. We all lived away from our childhood home by then.

One day in 1996, my brother, John, turned on the TV to watch *Everybody Loves Raymond*. The opening scene of the show was an image of the exterior of Raymond's house. John did a double take… that house looked *really* familiar, but he couldn't be certain. A little bit later, there it was again! "That looks like our house in Merrick," he thought. He called our mom. "I'm watching this show and I could swear I saw outside of your house." Mom was not much of a TV viewer and never found out when the show was airing on TV. So when John shared this observation with her, she was pleasantly surprised. "How nice! That must be the neighbor boy's show." Word spread quickly that our house was now featured on television as Ray Romano's house, and Marie and Frank's house was actually our neighbor's house from across the street!

I still enjoy watching reruns of that show, just to get a glimpse of our old house that holds so many memories for me. I remember traveling to Europe when airplanes had one big movie screen in the front. On our flight, they showed episodes of *Everybody Loves Raymond*. I excitedly stared at the screen and tried to resist the urge to point and yell out "Hey! That's *my* house!"

Grumman Aircraft Engineering Corporation / Grumman Aerospace Corporation

LEFT: The Grumman F4F Wildcat was built in the 1940s as a U.S. Navy aircraft. It was Grumman's first major warplane, a single-seat, single-engine carrier-based strike fighter, with a top speed of 318 mph. It was effective due to its maneuverability, long-range and ruggedness.
Photo courtesy of the Baldwin Historical Society and Museum.

Grumman Aircraft Engineering Corporation was founded by Leroy Randle 'Roy' Grumman on December 6, 1929, in Baldwin. Leroy Grumman was born in Huntington on January 4, 1895, and grew up on Long Island. Due to many seminal flights occurring on Long Island, including Charles Lindbergh's 1927 first transatlantic flight in a monoplane, by the mid-1920s the cluster of airfields on Long Island was dubbed the "Cradle of Aviation." The successful Lindbergh flight led to a rapid expansion in air travel and aircraft manufacturing.

World War II enhanced the need for military aircraft production. In 1932, Grumman received its first major U.S. Navy contract to build 27 two-seat FF-1 fighter planes. In 1937, Grumman increased its factory size and its workforce, and moved to a larger facility in Bethpage. By 1941, Grumman employed 6,500 people and continued to grow. To meet production demands during World War II, Grumman's workforce expanded at a rate of 1,000 workers per month. In September, 1943, the workforce peaked at 25,500 employees. The Grumman Corporation became one of the most important builders and producers of military and civilian aircraft in the 20th century.

ABOVE: Women production workers building a TBF Avenger, Grumman Aircraft, Bethpage, 1944. A leading supplier of Naval aircraft during World War II, approximately 40 per cent of Grumman Aircraft's workforce were women during the war. *Photo courtesy of the Cradle of Aviation Museum.*

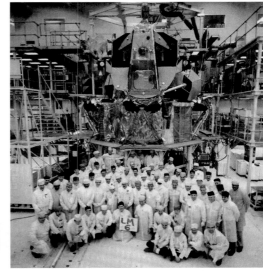

In 1961, President John F. Kennedy promised to land a man on the moon by the end of the decade. In 1962, Grumman was selected by the National Aeronautics and Space Administration (NASA), as the prime contractor for the Lunar Module (LM). In 1969, the Apollo 11 crew landed on the moon in the Grumman LM 5, and Neil Armstrong became the first man to step on the lunar surface. That year the name was changed to Grumman Aerospace Corporation.

Continuing into the 1980s, Grumman was the leading employer on Long Island. In 1986, it employed 23,000 people on Long Island and occupied 6,000,000 square feet in structures on 105 acres in Bethpage.

With the end of the Cold War at the beginning of the 1990s, reduced defense spending led to a wave of aerospace company mergers, including Grumman. In 1994, Grumman merged with the Northrop Corporation to form Northrop Grumman. That same year, the Long Island manufacturing facility, the last remaining location used for building military aircraft in the Northeast, was closed.

ABOVE LEFT: New Grumman F-14 Tomcats, Calverton, circa 1976. Grumman's other plant, in Calverton, was the site of final assembly and flight test of their aircraft from the late 1950s through the early 1990s. Their F-14 Tomcat was the greatest Naval jet fighter ever built.

ABOVE RIGHT: The "Clean Room" at Grumman, 1969. Grumman workers pose in front of a Project Apollo Lunar Module (LM-6/Apollo 12) in the Plant 5 Clean Room in Bethpage. Over 10,000 Long Islanders worked on the Apollo Program. **Every spacecraft that landed men on the moon was built by the hand of Long Islanders.**

BELOW: Softball game at Grumman Aircraft, Bethpage, 1945. Workers enjoy a lunch break ballgame, oblivious to the F6F Hellcats taxiing through the outfield. *Photos courtesy of the Cradle of Aviation Museum.*

The Coffee Pot and Bug Lighthouses, Orient Point

The Orient Point Lighthouse was constructed in 1899. It stands 64 feet tall and flashes a white light every five seconds. It is also known as "The Coffee Pot" Lighthouse.

The lighthouse is an active navigation aid standing at Orient Point in the Long Island Sound at the furthest point east on the North Fork of Long Island. It was constructed on Oyster Point Reef to help mariners navigate through Plum Gut, the area between the reef and Plum Island. It was restored in 1973, and upgraded in 1978 when the Plum Island Light was extinguished.

There is no public access to the lighthouse, but it is visible from the Orient Point/New London Ferry or from nearby land. It was added to the National Register of Historic Places in 2007.

TOP: The Coffee Pot Lighthouse. *Photo by Denise Rafkind.*

RIGHT: The Long Beach Bar (Bug Light) Lighthouse. *Photo courtesy of the United States Coast Guard.*

The Long Beach Bar Lighthouse sits off the western tip of Orient Beach State Park at the entrance to Orient Harbor. It was nicknamed the Bug Light because its original steel frame foundation made the light look like an insect. The original lighthouse constructed in 1870 was a two-story, wooden structure on a screwpile foundation, which in 1924 was updated to a reinforced concrete foundation. It was destroyed by arson in 1963. Currently what stands is a replica of plywood/vinyl siding shell, but the foundation was historically preserved. Today it remains an active maritime navigation aid.

Superstorm Sandy

On October 29 and 30, 2012, Superstorm Sandy hit Long Island. It was called a superstorm because as the tropical hurricane storm mixed with cooler air and made landfall, it maintained Category 1 hurricane strength, but lost its hurricane structure while retaining its intense winds of over 85 miles per hour. This created a storm surge on Long Island with its highest surges reported at 17.48 feet on the South Shore in Long Beach, and 12.45 feet on the North Shore in Kings Point. Sandy was the largest Atlantic storm ever recorded, covering an estimated 1,100 miles of the ocean and caused $62 billion in damage.

The effects of Sandy on Long Island were severe. Thousands of homes and businesses, along with 250,000 vehicles, were destroyed during the storm by flood or by fire.

Gasoline stations were closed or had no available fuel, rendering automobiles and trucks useless. The parking lots at Belmont Park in Elmont and Aqueduct Racetrack in South Ozone Park were used as "junk yards" for vehicles that were towed off the streets and highways. Homes and businesses would take months and in some cases years to be restored or rebuilt.

Photo courtesy of Newsday.

Cars buried in sand from Superstorm Sandy. Long Beach, November 7, 2012.
Photo by Andrea Booher, courtesy of FEMA and The U.S. National Archives.

Homeowners elevating their house above the new flood level of 12 feet, as determined by New York State and FEMA. Five 30-foot girders are placed under the house. Freeport, May 20, 2013.
Photo by Kenneth Wilsey, courtesy of The U.S. National Archives.

Fortunoff, Brooklyn and Westbury

ABOVE: Alan and Max Fortunoff, 1964.

LEFT: The interior of the Westbury store and the famous Flatware Wall, 1964.

In 1922, Max and Clara Fortunoff opened a neighborhood housewares store in Brooklyn, known for its value prices. The store would become a Brooklyn landmark. The chain grew to eight Fortunoff shops, all located under the elevated subway (referred to as "the el") on Livonia Avenue, East New York, Brooklyn. Max and Clara's children, Alan, Marjorie, and Lester, together with their spouses, Helene, Harry (Mayrock), and Lillian, all worked in the family business. The eight stores all developed different product lines and aspects of the market. In 1957, Alan's wife, Helene, introduced jewelry and watches to the Fortunoff store. In 1964, the Fortunoff and the Mayrock families consolidated the Brooklyn stores and moved to one "superstore" on Old Country Road in Westbury, Long Island.

The Long Island Fortunoff Store was known for its various departments. Faithful shoppers would remember the earliest departments such as records, gourmet foods, and cameras. Some of the departments grew or changed as the retail industry developed. Items that were always available, such as linens and bedding, rugs, lamps, art, tabletop, and fine gifts, were customer favorites. For decades, there was a Christmas Store that took over the entire lower level of the building from October to January.

fortunoff the source

It would be difficult to find a bride or groom on Long Island who did not either register with the Fortunoff Bridal Registry, or receive at least one bridal shower or wedding gift from Fortunoff. For decades, it was the go-to store for housewares, home furnishing, linens, jewelry, watches, and registry items such as crystal and china. The jewelry and watch department was celebrated for its retail selection of engagement and wedding rings, as well as its repair department.

Lester Fortunoff, Clara Fortunoff, Max Fortunoff, Marjorie Mayrock, Alan Fortunoff, 1972.

Expansion of the Fortunoff brand continued in the 1970s. Specialty jewelry stores opened on 5th Avenue in Manhattan and in New Jersey. In the 1980s, two full-line stores opened in New Jersey. In 1999, an internet-based shopping website and online bridal registry were launched. Marjorie Fortunoff-Mayrock, her husband Harry, and children Elliot, Rachel, and Isidore, developed a successful home division and all worked in the business.

In 2001, the Fortunoff Backyard Store was introduced. In 2005, the majority of the Fortunoff family interest was sold, and under the new owners in 2008, Fortunoff filed for bankruptcy. In 2009, the Fortunoff family reacquired the intellectual property of the company. The family licensed the name Fortunoff Backyard Store to a partner and now operates 14 locations in the Northeast.

In 2014, at the site of the original superstore, Fortunoff Fine Jewelry opened a boutique brick-and-mortar store on Old Country Road, in the Mall at the Source in Westbury. In 2021, Fortunoff Fine Jewelry closed the boutique to concentrate on building a bigger e-commerce business to meet the retail needs of the modern-day world.

Helene Fortunoff

Helene Fortunoff was a pioneering woman in the jewelry world who recognized the power and significance jewelry had for women. In 1957, she spearheaded the Fortunoff company's first entrance into the jewelry category. In 2000, after Alan Fortunoff died, Helene became the president of Fortunoff.

She was one of the first members of the Women's Jewelry Association (WJA) after its founding in 1983, recognizing that most women did not yet have a place at the table in jewelry businesses. She received WJA's Lifetime Achievement Award, and was one of the first recipients of National Jeweler Magazine's Hall of Fame designation for prominent retailers. Helene was the first woman invited to join the prestigious Carat Club, a diamond industry leadership group sponsored by De Beers. She served as chair for the Gemological Institute of America. In 1997, Helene Fortunoff received the honorary appointment as Knight of the Order of Merit of the Republic of Italy, in recognition of her long association and her assistance with Italian jewelry manufacturers.

She was a member of many boards of directors, both in the jewelry industry, and in her Long Island community. She served as chair of the board at Hofstra University. In October 2010, in recognition of her leadership and dedication, Hofstra renamed the Monroe Lecture Center Theater as The Helene Fortunoff Theater. Helene died in 2021, and her children, Esther and Ruth, continue as leading women in the jewelry industry.

Helene Fortunoff, pictured here with daughters Ruth and Esther, who both followed in her footsteps into the jewelry industry, 2002.

All photos courtesy of the Fortunoff family.

The Gold Coast Mansions

In the early 20th century, along the shoreline of the Long Island Sound, prominent American families built grand and elegant mansions. The affluence of the area caused it to be known as the "Gold Coast."

An estimated 500 mansions were built from 1890 to 1930. Their architectural styles included English Tudor, French Chateau, Georgian, Gothic, Mediterranean, Norman, Roman, Spanish, and various combinations thereof. Mansions resembled castles with towers upon lavish estates.

After World War II, many Gold Coast mansions were demolished. Estates were subdivided into today's suburban-style developments. It is estimated that only 200 of the original 500 mansions survived. Many were demolished; others were repurposed and renovated to be used as venues for special events and weddings. Some were converted into educational centers and museums.

Beacon Towers, Sands Point

Photo courtesy of The History Center, The Port Washington Public Library.

Beacon Towers was built in 1916. It was a 140-room Norman castle near the Sands Point Light. Its original owner was Alva Belmont, the former wife of William Kissam Vanderbilt. At the age of 46, Alva became the second wife of Oliver H. P. Belmont. Known for her numerous building projects, she commissioned a string of fantasy mansions on Long Island, Newport, Connecticut, and Manhattan. Funded by a $10 million settlement from her divorce from Vanderbilt and inheritance from Belmont, Beacon Towers was designed for Alva by architect Richard Howland Hunt.

Belmont named her residence Beacon Towers. It was extravagantly designed in French Châteaux style to resemble a fortified castle rising from the sea. The exterior was coated in smooth, gleaming white stucco. In 1924, Belmont bought the Sands Point Lighthouse property to keep the public off the sandy beach near her home.

Belmont sold Beacon Towers to William Randolph Hearst in 1927, who renamed it Hearst's Castle. Hearst sold the property in 1942 and it was demolished in 1945. Only segments of the walls and gatehouse survived.

It is believed that the Beacon Towers mansion served as inspiration for F. Scott Fitzgerald's 1925 novel *The Great Gatsby*.

INSET: Aerial view of both main buildings on the Guggenheim Estate, Hempstead House in the foreground, and the original residence Castle Gould. *Photo courtesy of The History Center, The Port Washington Public Library.*

LEFT: Castle Gould. *Photo courtesy of Creative Commons.*

The Guggenheim Estate,
Sands Point

Castle Gould was a 100,000-square-foot home built for Howard Gould in 1902 on his 106-acre estate. Gould was the son of railroad tycoon Jay Gould. The limestone building was designed by Richard Howland Hunt (1862-1931) in the style of Kilkenny Castle in Ireland.

Hempstead House, a 50,000-square-foot Tudor style mansion, was commissioned by Howard Gould in 1912 to placate his wife, who found the size of Castle Gould too large and impersonal. Hempstead house boasts 40 rooms and an imposing vaulted ceiling that incarnates the opulence and glamor of the roaring 1920s.

The couple divorced before Hempstead House was ever lived in and the property was sold in 1917 to Daniel Guggenheim. The property is also known as the Gould-Guggenheim Estate or Sands Point Preserve.

Falaise, the third mansion on the Guggenheim Estate, was built in 1923 by Daniel Guggenheim's son, Harry, on the 90 acres of the estate presented to him by his father upon his marriage. Falaise, which is the French word for cliff, is a waterfront, 13th century, Norman style manor. Falaise has an enclosed cobblestone courtyard, mortared brick walls, and a round tower. In 1939, Harry Guggenheim remarried to Alicia Patterson. Shortly thereafter, they founded *Newsday*, Long Island's daily newspaper. Falaise remains historically intact. The horse-head scene in *The Godfather* was filmed at Falaise.

After Daniel Guggenheim's death in 1930, his wife, Florence, closed off Hempstead House and built a small water-side home, which she named Mille Fleur. The property was later donated to Nassau County.

Sands Point Preserve, a non-profit institution, preserves and operates the four mansions of the estate. It has appeared as a location in numerous film and television shows, including *The Godfather* and *Gotham*.

The Sands Point Lighthouse

The Sands Point Lighthouse, the fourth lighthouse built on Long Island, stands 40 feet high. It was constructed in 1809. In 1924, socialite Alva Belmont purchased the Sands Point Light property at auction for $100,000. The property and lighthouse were sold to William Randolph Hearst in 1927 for $400,000. In 1942 Hearst sold the property which then remained in private ownership. On October 27, 1992, the Village of Sands Point and the Landmarks Commission designated the Lighthouse as a village landmark.

Photo by David Sharpe, courtesy of the Library of Congress.

Otto Kahn

Otto Hermann Kahn was born on February 21, 1867. He was a German-born, American investment banker, collector, philanthropist, and patron of the arts. In 1893, he accepted work in New York and spent the rest of his life in the United States. On January 8, 1896, Kahn married Addie Wolff. In 1917, Kahn gave up his British nationality and became a United States citizen.

His work included contracts with railroad builders and the reorganization of finances of the railroad systems. Kahn was a well-known figure, appeared on the cover of *Time Magazine* on November 2, 1925, and was sometimes referred to as the "King of New York." While his career was in banking, Kahn had always wanted to be a musician. He was a great patron of the arts, and served as the chairman of the Metropolitan Opera, vice president of the New York Philharmonic, and treasurer for the American Federation of Arts. Kahn co-founded the Federation of Jewish Philanthropies of New York.

Otto's son, Roger Wolfe Kahn, was a popular jazz musician and band leader of the late 1920s and early 1930s. Kahn's daughter, Margaret "Nin" Dorothy Wolff Kahn, married John Barry Ryan II and was a New York society doyenne and benefactor of the Metropolitan Opera.

LEFT: Otto Kahn (center) with actors Douglas Elton Fairbanks Sr. (left) and Charlie Chaplin.

LEFT: Addie Kahn with her four children: Maud (Momo) Emily Wolff Kahn, Margaret (Nin) Dorothy Wolff Kahn, Gilbert Wolff Kahn, and Roger Wolff Kahn.

ABOVE: The Maud Kahn Wedding at Oheka Castle. 1920.

Oheka Castle

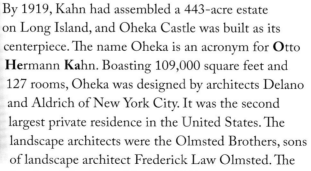

By 1919, Kahn had assembled a 443-acre estate on Long Island, and Oheka Castle was built as its centerpiece. The name Oheka is an acronym for **O**tto **He**rmann **Ka**hn. Boasting 109,000 square feet and 127 rooms, Oheka was designed by architects Delano and Aldrich of New York City. It was the second largest private residence in the United States. The landscape architects were the Olmsted Brothers, sons of landscape architect Frederick Law Olmsted. The estate was completed in time for his daughter Maud's wedding in 1920.

In the early 1900s, Khan had faced anti-Semitism. Social clubs had rejected Kahn's membership because he was Jewish. When he built his Oheka Castle at the highest point of Long Island's Gold Coast, he included his own golf course. The Oheka property also featured a working farm, a private airstrip, and numerous outbuildings.

TOP LEFT: The iconic main stairs of Oheka Castle, restored to their original beauty. *Photo by E Kaufman.*

LEFT INSET: The Eastern Military Academy Cadets on the main stairs of Oheka Castle. 1940s.

TOP: Library at Oheka, 2020s. *Photo by Brett Matthews.*

INSET: Library at Oheka, 1920s.

All photos courtesy of Oheka Castle.

ABOVE: An aerial view of Oheka Castle. 2020s.
Photo by Stephen Turner.

LEFT: Third Gatehouse, 1920s.

RIGHT: Rear elevation, 1920s.

Photos courtesy of Oheka Castle.

The Oheka Gardens and Reflecting Pool in the 2020s. They were in use as actual swimming pools in the 1920s.

Photo by Richard Nowitz Photography, courtesy of Oheka Castle.

Khan died on March 29, 1934. The property was sold to the City of New York for use as a retreat for sanitation workers and later, a government training school for merchant marine radio operators. In the late 1940s, an upscale housing development was constructed there and in 1948, the Eastern Military Academy (EMA) purchased the mansion and 23 surrounding acres.

By 1978, the school was bankrupt and the gardens bulldozed. Rooms were subdivided and the paneled walls painted over. Vandals repeatedly set fire to the building, but because Kahn had insisted on constructing a concrete, brick and steel structure, the house survived. In 1984, local developer, Gary Melius, purchased the estate for $1.5 million and began the largest private renovation project ever attempted in the United States. Unlike many of the mansions and estates that were lost, Oheka was beautifully restored, and today serves as a catering facility, restaurant, hotel, and conference center. Oheka Castle was added to the National Historic Register of Historic Places in 2004.

Joseph Lloyd Manor House,
Lloyd Harbor

In 1767, the Manor House was built for Joseph Lloyd (1716-1780) on the 3,000-acre provisioning plantation known as the Manor of Queens Village. The home was a Georgian style residence. It remained in the Lloyd family until 1876, eventually becoming the country house of Mrs. Anna Matheson Wood (1882–1980), who donated the property to Preservation Long Island in 1968.

The Joseph Lloyd Manor was the second house constructed on the plantation. The first, completed in 1711, was for his father, Henry Lloyd (1685-1763). The Henry Lloyd Manor House also survives and is located inside Caumsett State Park.

The Joseph Lloyd Manor House. *Photo by Historic American Buildings Survey, courtesy of the Library of Congress.*

Jupiter Hammon

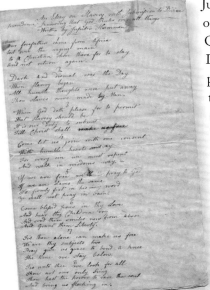

Jupiter Hammon was born into slavery on October 17, 1711, at the Manor of Queens Village in the home of Henry Lloyd. Hammon was one of many people of African descent enslaved at the Queens Village plantation. He served the Lloyd family his entire life, working under four generations of family masters. Hammon learned to read and write and was not only a servant in the house and on the farm, but he also assisted with the family's merchant business.

While enslaved at the Manor, Hammon wrote powerfully about the social and moral conflicts of slavery and freedom in the newly formed United States. Jupiter Hammon was the United States' first published African-American author, and is known as the founder of African-American literature. His earliest known poem, "An Evening Thought. [sic] Salvation by Christ with Penitential Cries," was published in 1761 when he was 50 years of age. Hammon's surviving writings consist of nine publications, 6 poems and 3 prose, and he became a leader in the African-American community. Hammon's date of death was unrecorded but is believed to be sometime before 1806.

The Joseph Lloyd Manor is recognized as a national Literary Landmark in honor of Jupiter Hammon. The Jupiter Hammon Project is a major initiative by Preservation Long Island, to develop a more relevant and equitable interpretation of Joseph Lloyd Manor, as a historic house and a site that enslaved generations of people of African descent.

LEFT: Shown here is a discovered poem, found in Hammon's own handwriting, "An Essay on Slavery, with submission to Divine providence, knowing that God Rules over all things," 1786.

Preservation Long Island was founded in 1948 as the Society for the Preservation of Long Island Antiquities, and changed names in 2017. It is a not-for-profit organization committed to working with Long Islanders to preserve its diverse cultural and architectural heritage through advocacy, education, and stewardship of historic sites and collections.

Jane's Carousel, Brooklyn

ABOVE: Jane's Carousel is housed in a pavilion that was commissioned by the Walentas, and designed by French architect Jean Nouvel, who is internationally renowned for his contemporary architecture in an urban context. The pavilion sits just off of the East River in Brooklyn. *Photos by Bill Barash.*

On September 16, 2011, Jane's Carousel opened to the public. Located off the East River in Brooklyn Bridge Park, it is a 48-horse, wooden carousel. It was constructed in 1922 by the Philadelphia Toboggan Company with horses carved by John Zalar and Frank Carretta. The carousel has 30 jumping horses, 18 standing horses, two chariots, and music provided by a Gebrüder Bruder Band Organ.

Until 1984, the carousel was at the Idora Park amusement park in Youngstown, Ohio and was called the Idora Park Merry-Go-Round.

It was purchased by real estate developer David Walentas and his wife, Jane Walentas, an artist. In her Brooklyn studio in DUMBO (the colloquial name for Down Under The Manhattan Bridge Overpass), Jane spent nearly two decades restoring the century-old carousel to its original beauty. She hand-scraped the wood, revealing the original 1922 color palette and wood carvings. Under carefully detailed renderings, the carousel was faithfully repaired, repainted, and placed at the Brooklyn Bridge Park.

William Llowyn Longyear

William Llowyn Longyear was born on June 17, 1899, in Manhasset. He was an illustrator, designer, author, and professor, best known for his work as a game artist and for his drawings of Long Island locations.

Longyear studied at the Art Students League, Columbia University, and the Pratt Institute. He worked at the Museum of Science and Industry in New York and as an illustrator at *Fortune Magazine*. In the 1930s, he designed board games, drew maps, and authored textbooks on advertising design and typography. By 1940, Longyear joined the faculty at Pratt Institute in Brooklyn, where he served as Chairman of the Department of Advertising Design and as Associate Dean. Longyear died on August 12, 1980.

ABOVE: William Longyear and his wife, Christine, on their honeymoon in 1924.

Selchow and Righter

Selchow and Righter, a 19th and 20th century game manufacturer, was headquartered in Bayshore and was best known for creating the games *Parcheesi* in 1870 and *Scrabble* in 1952. It was rare in the 1930s for board game artists to have name recognition on produced games, but William Longyear retained named credit for his designs of seven board games, including *Cargoes* and *Empires*.

Longyear's Long Island Drawings

Longyear was never without a pencil should he be inspired to sketch. His connection to Long Island was expressed in twelve pencil art drawings which he produced as promotional material. Entitled "Picturesque Long Island: Twelve Pencil Drawings for Framing by William Longyear, With the Compliments of Nesbit Oldsmobile, Inc. Manhasset," the drawings depicted Long Island places of interest.

LEFT: "Home Sweet Home" East Hampton Long Island, Birth Place John Howard Payne. Payne created the 1822 song "Home Sweet Home" with its lyrics "Be it ever so humble, there's no place like home."

Photos courtesy of Jim Polczynski and of the Longyear family.

Boardy Barn, Hampton Bays

On April 16, 1970, the Boardy Barn opened in Hampton Bays on West Montauk Highway, where Foxy's Worlds Famous Sandwiches once stood. With 4,000 square feet in the main building, and 12,000 square feet in the red and white tent and patio area, seating for 720 and 1488 standing, the Boardy Barn holds a place in the history of The Hamptons. The space was filled to capacity on Sundays from 3 p.m. until 8 p.m., from Memorial Day to Labor Day. It is rumored that they sold more beer in three months than Yankee Stadium sold in a full baseball season.

All photos courtesy of Boardy Barn.

For over five decades, owners Anthony (Tony) Galgano and Mickey Shields continued the summer tradition in the same location. In its early years, the Boardy Barn was a burger joint with live music. It had to close at 2 a.m. until the ordinance was changed to 4 a.m. The interior bars were the Square Bar and the Moose Bar, later called the Olde Towne Bar or the Malt Shop Bar. Back then, food was sold as well, although recently only hot dogs and pretzels were offered. Over the years it opened only on Sundays in the summer. On an average weekend, 1,500 to 2,000 people would visit the Boardy Barn. It was a happy place where people came to celebrate happy times, listen and sing along to the music they loved. The Boardy Barn motto says it all: "There's no strangers, just friends you haven't met."

A $20 cover charge gives access to $1 and $2 beers. Yellow happy face stickers adorn the patrons who may get a beer poured over their head as part of the revelry tradition. The popular watering hole has one rule; customers cannot wear orange, the color reserved for the security guards. Sadly, Anthony (Tony) Galgano died on November 20, 2021. Whether the Boardy Barn will reopen in 2022 is currently unknown.

Freemasonry on Long Island

Since 1793, Freemasonry has been active on Long Island. There were only 30 known members of the first Masonic Lodge in Huntington.

To attend meetings, members traveled many miles on foot, using a "ride and tie" method. Two Masonic brothers would start on their journey: one on foot and the other on horseback. The rider would reach a predetermined location first, tie the horse to a tree and continue to travel by foot. The walker would follow behind, eventually reaching the well-rested and tied horse, and gallop to the next planned rest stop. This continued until they each reached the lodge meeting. After an overnight stay, they returned home using the same method.

Freemasonry is veiled in allegory and illustrated by symbols. It is a society with secrets, but it is not a secretive society. Members have a shared belief of a supreme being, without prejudice of religious affiliation. At one point, Long Island was home to almost 80 Masonic Lodges. It is in these mysterious lodges and temples that well-dressed men would meet at night across Long Island.

ABOVE: The most famous Long Island Freemason is Theodore Roosevelt. He attained the degree of Master Mason in 1901 at Matinecock Lodge in Oyster Bay, less than three weeks after being sworn in as Vice President of the United States. *Photo courtesy of the Library of Congress.*

ABOVE: Originally constructed in 1875, pictured is the oldest Masonic lodge building in continuous active use in both the Suffolk and Nassau Masonic districts, Alcyone Lodge in Northport Village. *Photo courtesy of Alcyone Lodge and Ron Seifried.*

LEFT: The oldest active Masonic charter on Long Island belongs to Suffolk No. 60 in Port Jefferson, which first met in 1797. It traces its roots to Long Island's first Masonic Lodge, Huntington No. 26. Pictured is the Setauket Presbyterian Church as it appeared in 1912, when Suffolk No. 60 first moved into the 1854 structure, a place the lodge has called home for 110 years. *Photo courtesy of Suffolk No. 60 and Ron Seifried.*